*Profiles of African Leaders*

# Profiles of
# African Leaders

*THOMAS PATRICK MELADY*

*New York*
THE MACMILLAN COMPANY
A DIVISION OF THE CROWELL-COLLIER
PUBLISHING COMPANY
1962

*Fourth printing 1962*

The Macmillan Company, New York
Brett-Macmillan Ltd., Galt, Ontario

Printed in the United States of America

Library of Congress catalog card number: 61-5661

*This book about the leaders of Africa is affectionately dedicated to the people of Africa with the hope that their aspirations for a better life will be realized.*

# Preface

The historic drama that is taking place today in Africa has interested me since my graduate student days in the early 1950's. Since 1954 it has been my privilege to observe many aspects of this drama. I have visited most parts of Africa and discussed many contemporary political and economic topics with the African people.

The leaders of Africa have been of particular interest to me. Many of them have been generous enough in their time to review for me their hopes and aspirations for their peoples.

In these pages I have attempted to tell some things about nine African leaders, their peoples and their countries. While I have tried to relate the facts as I know them, it is also true that I still have the enthusiasm for Africa and Africans that I had in my school days.

Frequently I have been disappointed by the books on Africa because so few tell about the people. Here I have recounted some aspects of the leaders' lives that are not well known to the outside world and which when predicated against their country's background will give us a clear picture of the men.

I am grateful to many people in Africa and the United States for making this book possible. There are those individuals to whom I owe special thanks for their assistance: Mr. Charles A. Anger, Chairman of the Board, Consultants For Overseas Relations, Inc., for giving me the time off to make an extra trip to

West Africa in the winter of 1960 to obtain some data for this book; Miss Elizabeth Hunting Wheeler for her invaluable research assistance; Mr. Elliott Robbins for his searching editorial criticisms; and Mrs. Rose Fenton for faithful secretarial aid. To these friends, and many others, go my warmest thanks.

THOMAS PATRICK MELADY

New York
April, 1960

# Contents

# Special Note

Africa is a complex continent. While it is now united by the bond of the human determination of its peoples to live as equals with the rest of mankind, there are diverse peoples, languages and governments. Africa has been traditionally broken down into four basic areas.

1. Egypt and parts of neighboring Libya and Sudan. Here most of the approximately 34 million people speak Arabic, adhere to the Islamic faith, and have strong cultural, political and economic ties with the Middle East.

2. The Maghreb area, which includes Morocco, Algeria, Tunisia and part of Libya. Here also the language is Arabic and the religion of the overwhelming masses is Islamic. In Morocco, Algeria and Tunisia there have been strong French influences. In Algeria there is a strong European minority.

3. The Union of South Africa and the Rhodesias. Of the 21 million people in these two areas, 18 million are predominately Bantu. Slightly over 3 million whites control these two areas and have strong cultural ties with England and Holland. The official languages are English and Afrikaans.

4. Black Africa includes all of the continent below the Sahara except the Union of South Africa and the Rhodesias. The languages are diverse and the races are mixed Negro, Bantu and Hamitic. The population is a little more than 140 million people.

It is the fourth basic area of Africa that so few people know and appreciate. It is also the part of Africa which the author knows best. Consequently, in this book Black Africa is given the principal attention. It is this part of Africa where, beginning in 1957 in Ghana, the dramatic surge forward to independence has taken place. In these few short years new countries have appeared on the map, sometimes within a few days of each other.

A similar phenomenon has occurred with the leaders of this part of Africa. The men who are giving the leadership to these historical changes were, until these past few years, unknown even to the serious American student of international affairs.

# The African Revolution

When the end came for World War II, just four nations in the great continent of Africa could call themselves independent. Paradoxically, the nation with the longest uninterrupted record of self-rule had been established by former slaves. It also was the one African country to have direct links to the United States. Liberia, established in 1823, had gained recognition for its independence in 1847, almost a century before. It was also the first African country (by a few days) to be accepted as a member of the United Nations.

The Union of South Africa is, for the purposes of this book, a special case. It became a self-governing member of the British Commonwealth of Nations in 1910. At the time this book is written, however, the Union is embarked on a unique and, in the opinion of most of the world, a wrong-headed experiment bound for failure in its "apartheid" policy under which Black Africans are definitely second-class citizens.

Egypt for 175 years had been ruled by the Turks, French and English. It became an independent monarchy in 1922 when, a decent interval after World War I, the British passed control over to the dynasty that has been replaced by Gamal Abdel Nasser.

Ethiopia, also known as Abyssinia, had been a recognized member of the old League of Nations but had been seized by Mussolini's legions in 1935. Control was restored in the early part

*1*

of World War II to Emperor Haile Selassie I, who now holds the throne which has been in existence since Biblical times.

As soon as the world had overcome the paralysis induced by the wounds of war, an interval of about six years, the granting and taking of freedom by the various nations or territories of Africa began with the independence of Libya. It was not until five years later, however, that the real rush to independence started. The "Timetable of Independence" on pages 22 to 24 shows the progress that has been made.

## Size and Population

Africa is physically big. In contrast to South America's 7½ million square miles, Africa has 11½ million. It is also diverse. While there are thirteen countries in South America, including the three European-owned Guianas, the Dark Continent today can count approximately fifty different nations and territories.

Its 224 million people dwarf South America's 95 million or the 180 million of the United States. By contrast, while Africa is six times the geographic size of India, India has more than twice the population of Africa.

Africa produces most of the world's uranium, one-third of its chrome, one-sixth of its lead, three-quarters of its cobalt, 14 per cent of its tin, almost half of its antimony, over a third of its manganese and phosphates, almost a quarter of its copper, over 60 per cent of its gold and almost all of its precious diamonds. Africa's petroleum potential may be enormous. Her agricultural and hydroelectric resources have hardly been touched.

Despite the great political advances of the past few years and the widespread introduction of antibiotics, Africa is still plagued by most of the diseases known to mankind. The vast majority of the people are chronically undernourished. This problem has been intensified in areas where penicillin has drastically reduced infant mortality. The people are poorly clothed and housed. Africans own virtually no property. An overwhelming percentage of the people cannot read or write. Only five of at least seventy principal languages have their own indigenous written script.

## The Fight for Africa's Soul

For centuries a desultory war has been waged by the various branches of the Christian church to win the souls of Africa. To this has now been added the even more urgent proselytizing for Western-style freedom or Russian-sponsored communism. The combination of the struggle for freedom and political self-expression may precipitate a far more active interest in religion. Catholics, Protestants and Mohammedans are reaching out for the largely naturalistic souls of Africa. Islam, which went east and south as Christianity moved west, has an ancient tradition in Africa and its forces there are potent.

Africans will no longer be puppets. Much, however, is going on in the once Dark Continent that is being planned and guided by interests in London, Paris, Brussels, and Madrid which are liquidating or converting their colonies and spheres of influence there. Also in Washington and Moscow.

Russia, while it swiftly extinguished all thoughts of independence in Latvia, Lithuania and Estonia and has eliminated all but token nationality in Poland, Czechoslovakia, Hungary, Rumania, Bulgaria and Albania, has undertaken vast programs to facilitate Communist infiltration of the new nations of Africa.

Not only have trade fairs and economic missions descended on Egypt, Ghana and Guinea and other key points but the Soviets have taken themselves in hand to become African experts. Russian universities are making heroic efforts to build up authoritative African studies sections. The teaching of African sociology, art and customs is being developed. Particularly are the always linguistically-gifted Russians specializing in African languages. Special institutes have been organized to teach the basic tongues.

Russian museums are collecting authoritative exhibits of African art. Source materials are being developed for the use of students and Africanists. Soviet university libraries are being equipped with the best and most modern material on Africa available.

This concentration on basic African studies is both flattering to the African either in his own country or when he visits a festival or institute in Moscow or other behind-the-Iron-Curtain location. It is also intensely practical. Next to knowing your product the greatest secret of salesmanship is to know your customer.

Russia's "line" in Africa has ostensibly been to encourage independence, to stir anticolonial sentiment wherever it arose and to give covert encouragement to anything that would harass the European colonial powers. In the subtle international chess game, it is likely that this was a cover for Russia's real intentions which are not so much to obtain the freedom for Africa's people as to remove the stable authority of colonial rule. It is relatively easy, the Russians seem to have reasoned, to subvert the young, unstable, insecure and inexperienced new nation and gain control in an atmosphere of chaos. In the meantime, the European allies will have lost direct contact with and control of the vast resources of uranium, gold, silver, copper and oil that lie in Africa's mountains and deserts.

One of the most interesting questions to be answered in the years ahead is whether the Communists have actually served the interests of the Western world by the very encouragement that they have given to African independence. The colonial powers have moved out with really amazing speed. From the position where they have been constantly, indeed automatically, denounced for withholding liberty from subject peoples and exploiting the wealth of the continent, they have suddenly become old, too-distant friends with kindly paternal interest. The new countries of the world, not only in Africa but elsewhere, have sensed with the rapidity of a young person's instinctive fear of a too-friendly stranger, that communism is a form of outside control no less onerous and perhaps even more demanding than colonialism by a Christian and democratic nation.

Human nature, enforced by experience, has made new nations significantly reluctant to adopt either the forms or the symbols of dialectical materialism. Not so strangely, Africans like most everyone, love freedom. Most of them can be counted on to repel any system that has even an indirect threat of imposing a new slavery or control upon them.

Soon, the fortunate areas will find themselves being approached by rival bidders for their raw materials. As soon as Africa's 224 million people have climbed the first rung or two on the world economic ladder, they will find Europeans, Americans, Russians, Indians, Japanese and Chinese rapping on their door with goods to sell and deals to offer. For with the creation of markets must come the building of purchasing power through production. There could be a tremendously exciting and profitable time ahead for the African nations that are temperamentally suited to the self-discipline demanded by modern production methods—and blessed with the kind of government leaders who will permit, encourage and guide sound business and honest trade.

*Islam and Israel*

The granting of a homeland nation to the Jews of the world in their historic land of Israel has had what for most Westerners was an unlooked-for result. This was the reaction of Islam. Perhaps the extent and impact of this once terrifying military force has been reemphasized by the shrinking of the world or mankind's greater awareness of all the peoples of the earth. The rise of Pakistan, Indonesia and other Islamic countries is one of the significant facts of the present day.

While not a part of Africa, the proclamation of Israel as an independent state on May 14, 1948, exerted a strong, stimulating influence not only on the Moslem people themselves but on the

leading powers who were susceptible to Moslem competitive per-
suasion or had important interests involving oil and other raw
materials located in Islamic countries.

In Africa, the existence of large Moslem groups in many of the
new nations seems to come as a surprise to Americans and other
Westerners.

Islam stands as a potential challenge to Christianity and, of
course, Christianity challenges Islam. Unlike the confrontation at
the time of the Crusades, today's rivalry has been peaceful, so
far. Perhaps here is another example of that situation so well described by Toynbee in his *Study of History*—a "challenge and
response." The vitality and will to live of these two great re-
ligions can be demonstrated by their reaction to this situation
with a large, uncommitted majority that is now one of the religious facts of life in Africa.

## Who Will Lead?

One of the great questions of history is whether situations make
leaders or whether it is the completely accidental appearance of
a certain man that makes history go one way or another. Would
there have been a World War II without Hitler? Would the
United States now be part of the British Commonwealth if it had
not been for Washington, Jefferson and Adams? Why have Spain
and Portugal been largely dormant for three hundred years?

Would Ghana be a leading new Republic in Africa without
Nkrumah? This is not to spin out idle questions but rather to em-
phasize the vast importance of the individual—one man—in the
history of a state or continent.

Until a few years ago, an American college student if he knew
anything at all about Africa would have known something about
its raw materials, its geography, perhaps something of the slave
trade and the spheres of influence carved out by the European
powers in the nineteenth century. The contrast with today is
complete. American college men and women now are mingling

with African exchange students in their classes. Visiting African experts attract large and attentive audiences of American citizens who turn out to hear the speeches of African leaders coming to this country.

Great changes in form are now in progress and there is no doubt that many more changes in the basic nature of the continent are evolving.

The African people themselves have been and will continue to be responsible for much of these changes. The Moslem areas of North Africa were among the first to trigger the demand for independence, with Libya, Sudan, Morocco and Tunisia leading the way.

Great Britain, the foremost colonizer of the world and parent of most of the world's major democracies, decided once North Africa was free to lead off with the granting of independence to its colony and protectorate, the Gold Coast, located in the center of the southern coast of Africa's westward bulge.

The inhabitants, under the colorful leadership of President Kwame Nkrumah, selected the ancient African name of Ghana. As the first Negro African nation to free itself from European rule, Ghana's black star provided dramatic impetus to nationalist movements among the newly awakened African people. The hundreds of thousands of Ghanaian people in Accra who sang the chorus line of "Freedom" with tears flooding their eyes on the historic day, March 6, 1957, were a dramatic proof, so long denied, that black Africans could emerge from subjection to rule themselves.

### De Gaulle's Four Choices

The postwar campaign by Soviet Russia against "colonialism" was nevertheless effective enough to create great self-distrust among the two largest colonial powers, Britain and France. With the advent of de Gaulle, however, a startling and positive development took place in the French-controlled nations.

Exhibiting once more that touch of originality and genius that is the mark of a true historic figure, de Gaulle hit upon the plan of offering a choice to France's African possessions. By simple vote they could choose one of four alternatives:

1. They could become an integral part or departments of France, with representation in the French Chamber of Deputies.

2. They could retain their position as overseas territories.

3. They could become autonomous, self-governing nations within the newly-created French Community of Nations which replaced the French Union that had been set up in 1946.

4. They could vote themselves out of the French orbit entirely and depart in peace.

Following strenuous preparations which took into account that millions of the voters would be completely illiterate, the balloting began in the fall of 1958.

Twelve of the colonies voted to become autonomous African republics and two voted to become overseas territories of France. Guinea alone voted to become wholly separated from France. While this may be regarded as a slap at French rule or even at France herself, Guinea's action actually validated the whole election. It proved that there was no trick, that a country could, and indeed did, vote itself right out of any control or relationship with France and become an independent, separate nation.

By the end of 1960 the twelve autonomous African republics had, with the cooperation of France, become independent, sovereign states. The majority of these states have entered into agreements with France and the Community. The others are in the process of negotiating these agreements.

France's President Charles de Gaulle in a few short years destroyed most of the opprobrium of colonialism in all of France's ex-colonies with the exception of Guinea. While the exact nature of the Community is, at this early point in its development, difficult to define from a juridical viewpoint, there is good indication that these twelve states will freely remain, as sovereign members, in the Community.

The French African territories that voted to become self-governing autonomous republics in 1958 and obtained full independence and sovereignty by the end of 1960 were:

| | |
|---|---|
| Republic of Chad | Malagasy Republic |
| Central African Republic | Republic of Mali |
| Republic of Congo | The Islamic Republic of Mauretania |
| Republic of Dahomey | Republic of the Niger |
| Gabon Republic | Republic of Senegal |
| Republic of the Ivory Coast | Voltaic Republic |

The Cameroon and Togoland areas administered by the French as United Nations Trusteeship areas were given their independence in early 1960. Both these states have close relationships with France and the Community states.

*Changing Boundaries*

In the process of obtaining their independence, the former French Sudan and Senegal formed the Federation of Mali. On June 20, 1960, the Federation of Mali received its independence from France. However, within two months, Senegal had seceded from the Federation and declared her independence as the Republic of Senegal. This left the Soudanese Republic as the only remaining member of the Mali Federation. In September, 1960, the Soudanese Republic, recognizing that the Federation was no longer possible, proclaimed its independence as the Republic of Mali.

Ivory Coast, Dahomey, Niger and the Voltaic Republic have formed the Council of the Entente. A cooperative association of sovereign states, the Council seems now to be the most successful of the several groupings of states attempted in Africa.

Other discussions of combinations or unions of one sort or another have taken place. President Tubman of Liberia has urged trade treaties and joint cooperative efforts wherever such would be beneficial to the nations concerned.

There is little question that combination, or split-ups, of present territories and countries are going to occur in the future. Africa will indeed be fortunate if it can avoid the endless boundary disputes of Europe and bloody tragedies like South America's Chaco War.

*Belgian Areas*

In the heart of sub-Sahara Africa lies the huge Congo. This is the great Belgian territory that Emperor Leopold II took over almost as his private preserve in the 1870's. Sir Henry Stanley, who had proved his skill and leadership by finding Dr. Livingstone, returned to make extensive explorations in the Congo and his name is memorialized in Stanley Falls and Stanleyville. The outside world has heard little of what went on inside the Congo, but changes in local government forms were effected in 1957 and again in 1959. With all the progress in British and French territories, the uneasy Belgians enunciated a new plan pointing toward "democracy" in the Congo that would make it "capable of exercising sovereignty in making decisions about its independence."

The nationalist pressures of 1959 and 1960 increased the likelihood of major constitutional change. After an effective boycott of local elections in 1959 on the eve of King Baudouin's arrival in Leopoldville, the five nationalist parties called for "complete, immediate and unconditional independence."

Following the king's December, 1959, visit, major discussions in Brussels resulted in the dramatic announcement that the Congo would become independent on June 30, 1960.

Shortly after the former Belgian Congo became the Republic of the Congo on June 30, 1960, there were severe riots and civil disorder in various parts of the new republic. The summer months of 1960 were tragic ones for the Congolese and Belgian peoples. Hundreds were killed. The country was divided and in a state of shock and paralysis.

The United Nations played the key role in restoring a minimum level of order. It is of course premature to discuss the causes of the Congo difficulties in this book. The author would, however, like to offer two comments: when the Congo received its independence there were not more than a dozen University graduates for a country with almost 14 million people. In the rush for independence that has swept Africa the Congo is the only independent state where serious, prolonged civil disorders took place.

Between the ex-Belgian Congo and Tanganyika lies Ruanda-Urundi. From 1878 to 1918 this was a part of German East Africa. The small, adjoining kingdoms of Ruanda and Urundi were mandated to Belgium by the League of Nations. In 1946 they were made a United Nations Trust Territory under Belgian administration. In Ruanda in November, 1959, the Watusi, the immensely tall and athletic peoples seen by American motion picture goers in *King Solomon's Mines* and other pictures, and the Bahutu tribes renewed an old conflict. Over a hundred lives were lost. In the course of the emergency, Belgium announced a plan whereby Ruanda-Urundi would be less subordinated to the Belgian Congo. Separate elections in Ruanda and Urundi are in view.

### Portuguese Areas

Two of the areas that are among the least talked about in Africa are the relatively quiet Portuguese areas of Angola—a territory of almost half a million square miles on the Atlantic Coast just under Congo—and Mozambique, a territory opposite the Malagasy Republic (Madagascar) on the East Coast.

Portugal also controls Portuguese Guinea, between Senegal and French Guinea.

### Spanish Areas

Spain has already ceded Spanish Morocco to the nation of Morocco. Its major areas today are the Spanish Sahara and the city of Ifni.

The outside world is important to Africa. It is well understood that there are many techniques—of manufacturing, agriculture and animal husbandry, products and devices of an astonishing variety, fields of education and knowledge, that other nations can bring to Africa. There is also the matter of man's religion and his view of life. The moral and economic system that the African chooses to live under will have fundamental effects on his freedom and well-being. No one denies that progress and self-government in Africa will require immense amounts of work, nor that Africans are able and willing to work. For a century or two, Africans have worked not so much for themselves as for colonial or perhaps tribal rulers. How much harder the African will work when he learns that what he makes belongs to him for his own enjoyment and that of his family; that by being ingenious, by saving a little something for tools or perhaps special education, he can make far more in the end than if he spends it all the day he earns it. This is the great secret that has unlocked the wealth-creating energies of men—whether they were white, yellow or black.

Africa has vital materials, not only the uranium and chrome of the Congo, the oil of the Sahara, the gold and diamonds of the Rhodesias and Tanganyika, but both raw materials and the finished goods to come that will develop from Africa's new energy and skills. Africa can offer markets for many products which the West has in abundance. But there are several problems.

Just before taking the plane at one of the East African capitals, I ran into a young businessman. He was a Frenchman but he had some experience in other parts of the world. He told me of a South Sea island he had recently come from which illustrated, he suggested, something that might happen in some sections of Africa. There were about twenty thousand Polynesians on the island around sixty years ago. At that time two Chinese families, driven out by the Boxer Rebellion, arrived on the island and set up small shops. Today, he said, the Chinese, by natural increase and the immigration of relatives, number twelve thousand. More astonishing, they now own all the shops and the small factories on the island. The Polynesians are resentful. "We owned this island, once. Now we just work as waiters in the restaurants or hands in the factories," a Polynesian told him.

Centuries of business experience have given the Chinese an almost innate business ability. This is something that may come hard to many Africans. It is a skill that must be learned if African nations are to develop modern industry and achieve significantly higher living standards. Not everyone can be a political leader, or a professor.

At the moment, any attempt to produce manufactured goods and, particularly, any project to produce for export, represents what can only be called a bold venture. But it could come. Given the will to achieve a certain standard of living, the techniques that can be imported and learned, Africa need not remain solely a source of raw materials.

This is the critical and climactic moment of birth for many new nations and for emerging cultures. Their new beginnings will affect their history as surely as the Declaration of Independence and the Constitution have been guides for the United States. This is the time; and it is here that I shall seek to tell, each in his proper setting, of the men.

## II

## *Africa: The Birth of Leadership*

The nature of Africa's new leaders provides the most important single clue not only to the explosive forces at work but to the nature of the often diverse people of Africa themselves. Heroes and hero worship, though muted by the civilizing forces of modern society, still provide the great dynamic for change. Africa, once the "Dark" Continent, is now the Changing Continent.

The last two hundred years of world history offer glowing examples of one man's power to bring freedom and wanted changes to his people. Each leader draws strength from the land and people from which he springs but each gives of his own character and personality to stimulate others and forge the nature of the new state. George Washington led a volunteer army of farmers and tradesmen against the armies of the most powerful empire of his time. It was his tenacity and generalship that held the scattered settlements together and won the victory but only his character created the atmosphere of trust that helped bring agreement on the Constitution and the essential strengthening of the government that made survival possible.

In South America in the 1820's, the immense revolution against Spain was chiefly inspired and led by Simón Bolívar who combined in his single genius the combativeness, generalship and political skill that led to independence. Though his heart was broken by his inability to create in effect a United States of South

14

America, the virtuosity of Bolívar's sword and pen won him a sacred place in the heart of a continent's people.

Abraham Lincoln, so often revered for his gentleness, did not hesitate to lead his country into war and fight through to victory to preserve the Union, at the opportune moment cutting out the cancer of slavery. Under his leadership, the nation solved a problem that had baffled the efforts of lesser men for generations.

In Asia, Sun Yat-sen, born to Christian parents, plotted the overthrow of the crumbling Manchu dynasty. After extensive efforts and long exile, he organized the prorepublican Kuomintang which eventually won control of the country. He served briefly as president of South China. Knowing the nature of his people, he used ruthless methods in eliminating opposition. He left his mark upon the country and even before his death had become known as the Father of the Chinese Republic.

The Middle East boasts no greater modern figure than Kemal Ataturk, the doughty Turkish general who transformed his defeated country after World War I. Taking over its government in 1920, he first drove the Greeks out of Asia Minor, established a republic and ended the caliphate. These changes merely set the stage for more. Ataturk abolished polygamy, decreed an end to the veil for women and the fez for men. He not only introduced Western dress but, more important, changed the alphabet to conform to Western usage.

India's greatest leader is a unique contribution to history— Gandhi, the crusader for nonviolence in a violent century. The Mahatma's career had African origins, as his first campaign against discrimination due to race began in Natal where he was a young lawyer. That Gandhi could exist and revolt successfully against the British was attributable not only to his own skill but to the restraint of the authorities and Britain's reluctance to use more direct means of suppression. One can only imagine the ghastly results of a campaign of "passive resistance" in a modern Communist state.

Africa, since 1946, has required unusual skill in diplomatic negotiations, debating and in human relations. The African leaders with the spotlight of world opinion upon them have pleaded their cause before the United Nations, at international conferences and in the major capitals of the world. Few present leaders of Western nations have gone through such exhaustive workouts in the court of world opinion.

Those of us who have attended United Nations' meetings have been deeply moved by the determination of African leaders to obtain the goals of their people. Despite this glowing determination and idealism, some have already had the opportunity to show restraint in victory as well as in defeat.

Those familiar with the history of Europe's "mad scramble" for choice sections of Africa in the nineteenth century stand amazed at the ability of African leaders to "forgive and forget." When His Imperial Majesty Haile Selassie I entered Addis Ababa with his army of liberation on May 4, 1941, he called on the Ethiopians to thank God for their freedom and to forgive the Italian people. The hundreds of thousands of Italian colonists and soldiers who were turned over to the Ethiopian Army in 1941 received from the Ethiopian people a Christian charity which the Fascist occupation forces never showed to the Ethiopians.

## Leadership in Africa

Destiny has now thrown the spotlight on Africa. It is aglow with the light of joyous and determined peoples rushing to obtain political goals that have been beyond their reach until the last few years. Behind the shouting and dancing had long lurked a great determination to be free.

The year 1946 marked the start of the big change in Africa. At that time the outside public was acquainted with the names of only a few leaders in Africa. As far as sub-Sahara Africa was concerned the only known figures were possibly Ethiopia's Haile

Selassie and Liberia's President Tubman. Since the rush for independence the list of names known to the public has expanded to include Kenya's Tom Mboya, Tanganyika's Julius Nyerere, Senegal's Léopold Senghor, Guinea's Sékou Touré, Ghana's Kwame Nkrumah, Ivory Coast's Félix Houphouet-Boigny, Nigeria's Prime Minister Sir Alhaji Abubakar, Cameroon's Amadou Ahidjo, and a small handful of others.

## Now the World Is on Their Side

In 1823 a new African state was born. A group of ex-slaves had courageously left the United States, crossed the dangerous Atlantic and settled on West African shores. The leaders had nothing except their courage and love of freedom to sustain them. No one outside of a handful of American churchmen did anything to help them solve their nearly insurmountable problems.

Today the newly independent countries still face many of the same difficulties that almost extinguished the Liberian nation: poverty, disease, illiteracy and lack of national unity. But the great change today is that world opinion is now on the side of the African people. Powerful international organizations like the United Nations and private world humanitarian groups are waiting to help them. These also are important factors in the equation necessary to develop dynamic, well trained political leaders.

The emergence of a high level African leadership élite is a reality of today's world. When the tide of independence spread to African sub-Sahara there were dire predictions of catastrophe —some even predicted that millions of Africans would be killed or injured in the chaos that would occur when the European powers no longer had full governing authority. These predictions were far from groundless, as most changes in the political status of peoples have been accompanied by bloodshed. The four great instances of sudden political change for large numbers of peoples of the past two hundred years occurred when the North American, South American, French and Russian peoples broke with their colonial masters or their own governing class and formed a new, drastically different social and political society. Each of these revolutions brought violence and death.

Amazingly the special characteristic of the political changes that have occurred in Africa since 1946 is their relative absence of bloodshed and civil disorder. This, of course, reflects favorably both upon the African people and on the European powers concerned.

The exceptions to the nonviolent changes taking place in most of Africa have been the areas where the transition to real local autonomy for Africans has been slow. In the long period of Belgian rule in the Congo, the first steps toward developing a politically experienced leadership group were not taken until 1957—just three years before the country became independent! The recent tragedies in the Union of South Africa which have caused death and bloodshed certainly have not been caused by Negro Africans.

The wrong kind of leadership in African countries that are now independent could have guided their people into mass excesses in the moment of the emotional peak of freedom at long last realized.

### The New Generation

A tremendous social change in Africa has taken place among the younger people. Here again, the change has been caused by the two major political developments affecting Africa: the rush of the African peoples toward independence and the struggle that has emerged in the last few years for their minds and their hearts.

The young people, while not participating directly in contemporary political developments, have been overtaken by the sense of urgency to leap over the centuries of inactivity and catch up with the rest of the world in a few years. In their case, the rush has been for education. Africa has hundreds of thousands of young men and women between fifteen and twenty-five whose parents were by technical standards illiterate and who lived in a tribal or village situation. These young men and a few women receive their initial elementary education near their birthplace, and now they have been psychologically and physically separated from their homes. In most cases they wander into the urban centers of their countries where they seek more advanced education or employment.

They have lost or rejected the value system of their parents. This, coupled with the disintegration of Africa's traditional tribal society, has resulted in most of them living in a political vacuum, but at the same time they are possessed with a drive to bring quick solutions to the age-old problems that have afflicted their peoples, problems not only of political independence but also the great scourges of Africa—poverty, disease and illiteracy.

New leadership demands that there be followers; not merely some who can applaud the triumphs but those who can and will do the work that will help make genuine progress possible. Africa's future depends on young people—like a young Ethiopian boy named Tecle—"Tec" for short. Tec is a common name among Ethiopian boys, just as Joe is here in America.

## The Struggle of Tec

Several years ago in a village in southeastern Ethiopia, Tec heard that in the capital city of Addis Ababa there were schools for advanced learning and if he were not admitted to one of these schools there were still libraries where he could read books, newspapers and magazines. Tec, though born into a tribal Ethiopian family where both his mother and father were technically illiterate, had received his elementary and some high-school education in neighboring missionary schools. When he completed this schooling he was not prepared psychologically to return to the pastoral life of his family. He determined to go to Addis Ababa where more education either at schools or libraries was possible.

With his few clothes in hand, this nineteen-year-old boy set out on the six-hundred-mile trek to the capital of his country. He caught rides when he could, sold most of his clothes so that he could eat, and walked—and walked—and walked. Having gone without food for the last two days of his journey, he arrived in Addis Ababa so weak that he had to be sent to a hospital.

After a week of treatment, food and rest, Tec began to visit the principal libraries of the city. He would arrive when the library opened and remain there until it closed, taking time out only for his meals. After six months of this seven-days-a-week schedule, he was admitted to the Ethiopian Agricultural College.

Tec is the living symbol of African youth. They will walk hundreds of miles to read a few books, to learn of the heritage of the past and to catch up on the great technological progress made by the rest of the world. They will go without food and clothes in order to drink at this fountain of knowledge. The sacrifices being made by African young people for advanced education is an example of the young people in the world rising to a great challenge.

The unfortunate fact is that this noble passion of African youth to obtain education has occurred simultaneously with the destruction of their own value system and the appearance of Soviet communism, which demands only two things from the African—his mind and his heart. The decade 1960 to 1970 will tell the story of whether the young people of Africa can be successful in learning twentieth century technology without falling victims to the camouflaged colonialism of the Soviets.

The complexion of overseas rule that once directed the affairs of the African people has changed. With a few exceptions the European powers have withdrawn from the active direction of internal African affairs. A subtle change in the type of colonialism being offered the African peoples has occurred in the past few years. Soviet communism, under the cloak of the Marxist value system, which is associated with dramatic improvement in the standard of living of the Russian people, is the new colonialism being offered the African peoples. The Soviets claim that their system can bring the same alleged wonders for the African people that it brought for the Russian people. That Moscow would ultimately seek to control the system is ignored.

In this case, of course, the new system is a drastic change. The old colonialism demanded that the African areas fit into the trade development programs of their European administrators. Local political development leading to autonomy within varying frameworks was allowed to take place. The new colonialism, however, demands absolute allegiance to its political value system. It demands the unquestioning allegiance of the minds and the hearts of the African people rather than the commitment of their land and raw material. The African people have not indicated that they wish to change from European domination to Marxist socialism controlled by Moscow.

The third significant change on the African scene has been with the young people. We see African youth rushing to bring quick change to the social and economic situation in which they and their people live. These young Africans, some of whom will be the leaders of tomorrow, are possessed with an overpowering determination to do whatever is necessary to bring the fruits of modern civilization to their people.

Dramatic social and political changes have taken place in Africa since 1946. Mature leadership in Africa has played a leading role in making these changes possible.

When the great hour of freedom struck for the African people there was a rush of frenzied activity to bring about self-government as soon as possible. In this dash for freedom a great majority of African leaders silhouetted themselves as capable, mature, determined men who would match the quality of leaders who have led other peoples at other times to freedom. In the next few chapters we shall take a close look at some of these leaders who have been in the forefront of African independence activities in the past few years.

## Timetable of African Independence

1. Ethiopia

Except for brief periods in its early history, has always been an independent monarchy except during the Italian occupation, 1936–1941.

2. Liberia

Organized by American missionaries for former slaves from the United States; established in 1823.

3. Egypt

An independent country since 1922. The unity of Egypt has existed over the known six to seven millennia. In modern times Egypt has been ruled by the Ottoman Empire, France and the United Kingdom.

4. United Kingdom of Libya

Was the first country to obtain independence through the direct action of the United Nations. Libya was under Carthage, Rome, the Vandals, the Turks, the Italians, the United Nations until it received independence on December 24, 1951.

5. Republic of Sudan

Under an Anglo-Egyptian administration until January 1, 1956, when independence was obtained.

6. Morocco

A remnant of the Shereefian Empire of the seventh century. A French protectorate from 1911. Received independence on March 2, 1956.

7. Tunisia

Formerly a Barbary state under Turkey. From 1881–1957 a French protectorate. Became a republic on March 20, 1956.

8. Ghana

Formerly the Gold Coast. Ghana's receiving independence from the United Kingdom on March 6,

| | |
|---|---|
| | 1957, signaled the push for independence in Black Africa. |
| 9. Republic of Guinea | Voted self out of the French Community on September 28, 1958, and became independent on the following October 2nd. |
| 10. Republic of the Cameroons | Formerly a German colony. After World War I it came under the League of Nations and later under the United Nations with part French and part British administrations. The French part became independent on January 1, 1960. |
| 11. The Republic of Togo | On April 27, 1960, the French administered part of the United Nations trusteeship area of Togoland became independent. |
| 12. Malagasy Republic | Formerly Madagascar. A French protectorate from 1885; became an autonomous republic in the French Community in October, 1958; later in June, 1960, an independent state still associated with the Community. |
| 13. Republic of the Congo | The former Belgian colony obtained its independence on June 30, 1960. |
| 14. Somali Republic | The former Italian UN Trusteeship area of Somalia and British Somaliland became one independent nation on July 1, 1960. |
| 15. Republic of Dahomey <br> 16. Republic of Niger <br> 17. Voltaic Republic <br> 18. Republic of the Ivory Coast <br> 19. Republic of Chad <br> 20. Central African Republic <br> 21. Republic of Congo <br> 22. Gabon Republic <br> 23. Islamic Republic of Mauretania | Former colonies, protectorates or territories of France which, in November or December, 1958, became autonomous republics in the French Community; and independent states by the end of 1960. |

24. Republic of Senegal

In November, 1959, Senegal became an autonomous republic in the French Community; subsequently in June, 1960, uniting with the Sudan Republic into the Mali Federation. In August, 1960, Senegal withdrew from the Federation and declared its independence.

25. Republic of Mali

A French colony, it became the Sudan Republic, an autonomous republic within the Community. In June, 1960, linked to Senegal in the Mali Federation as a member of the Federation, it became independent. In September, 1960, after Senegal had withdrawn from the Federation in August, 1960, the country known as the Sudan Republic declared its independence as the Republic of Mali.

26. Federation of Nigeria

The former British colony and protectorate became independent on October 1, 1960.

27. Tanganyika

Formerly German East Africa, it became a British Trust Territory in 1919. Local self-rule given in late 1960; independence in the near future.

28. Kenya

A British crown colony which in February, 1960, received a promise of early independence.

29. Sierra Leone

A British colony and protectorate which will receive its independence in April, 1961.

# III

## Haile Selassie I—
## The Elder Statesman

Ethiopia holds the proud distinction of being both one of the larger nations of Africa and the one with by far the longest record of independence. For centuries stretching back to Biblical times, Ethiopia (sometimes called Abyssinia) has had the benefit not only of geographic inaccessibility but outstanding rulers including the Queen of Sheba, the legendary Prester John and the no less heroic figure of today's Haile Selassie I.

Leadership has played a historic role here. It inspired a successful defense against the Islamic advance that swept irresistibly across other great areas of Central and East Africa. Ethiopia later achieved the unique honor of being the only African nation to survive attack in 1896 and defeat a European nation during the nineteenth century "mad scramble" to carve up the continent.

The same combination of fierce patriotism combined with high moral purpose shocked an apathetic world in 1936 when His Imperial Majesty Haile Selassie I challenged the conscience of the world to condemn the Fascist rape of his people. The world was too preoccupied with its depression worries and the threat of war to heed his heroic message before the League of Nations but within six years Haile Selassie was to enter Addis Ababa with an Allied army of liberation. His proclamation to his people called not for revenge but for Christian charity toward the now

25

conquered Italian invaders—despite their record of atrocities and the use of poison gas. Today Haile Selassie continues to show that dynamic material progress can take place without doing violence to the ancient traditions of the African people.

### Ethiopia—An Ancient Land; A Sturdy People

The empire of Ethiopia comprises the country of Ethiopia proper plus, today, the former Italian colony of Eritrea. Located in northeastern Africa, it is bounded on the north by the Red Sea, on the west by the Sudan, on the south by Kenya and Somalia and on the east by British and French Somaliland. The country covers 395,000 square miles—an area equal to that of Texas, Kansas and Oklahoma combined. High plateaus topped by lofty mountain ranges characterize the topography of Ethiopia. The Rift Valley cuts across the country in a general northeastern-southwestern direction, separating the Ethiopian high plateau to the west from the Somalia plateau to the east. Most of the principal cities are high above sea level on higher portions of the Ethiopian plateau, including Addis Ababa, the capital, 8,000 feet, Asmara, capital of Eritrea, 7,640 feet and Jimma, 5,575 feet. The Ogaden, a semidesert located in the lower levels of the Somali plateau, occupies the entire southeastern part of the country. In this way, topography provides Ethiopia with a built-in defense perimeter which was invaluable in defending her independence against the Moslems in the fifteenth century and against the Europeans in the nineteenth century.

The highlands of the empire have a temperate climate. In Addis Ababa and Asmara, for example, the average is around 62° F. This climate, so unlike the tropical heat of equatorial Africa, has been a contributing factor to the early development of the Ethiopian state.

The rainfall pattern is concentrated in the "heavy" and "little" rainy season each year. Actually, both rainy seasons almost merge into a single season of varying duration over most of the empire.

The rains usually start during April or May and end in September. The dry season lasts from October to March. The rainfall averages about 48 inches annually in Addis Ababa and 25 inches annually in Asmara, and this factor coupled with fertile land in a temperate climate assures Ethiopia sufficient food production for her peoples.

The native population is about 15 million. Addis Ababa is estimated to have around 500,000; Asmara 100,000 and Dessi 40,-000. Most of the leading towns range in population from 5,000 to 20,000. The majority of Ethiopians live in their tribal environment and devote themselves to agriculture. However, it is the less than a million Ethiopians who live in the principal urban centers who constitute the politically conscious élite.

As far as ethnic background is concerned, most Ethiopians are of Hamitic or Hamitic-Semitic stock, but there are some Negroid tribes in the west and southwest. Foreigners number less than fifty thousand and are mostly Arabs, Indians, Italians, Greeks and Armenians.

Tradition says that the Semitic tribes from southern Arabia crossed the Red Sea and settled in the land of the Cush. These tribes spoke a language related to Hebrew and Arabic. They were cultured people and brought with them the Sabaean alphabet, still in universal use in today's Ethiopia, although in modified form. These Arabian tribes migrating to the highland and intermingling with the highland Hamites residing there are the ancestors of the present-day Ethiopians of the plateau. There are two main Cushite groups: those of the highlands and those of the lowlands.

The diverse ethnological background is matched by the diversity of languages and dialects in Ethiopia. There are some forty native languages and dialects in Ethiopia, all belonging to one of the three main language groups: Hamitic, Hamitic-Semitic and Nilotic Negro. The principal written languages are Amharic, the most important language and one of the official languages of the empire, and Tigre, one of the official languages of Eritrea. The Galla language is second in importance in Ethiopia. English is now the second official language of Ethiopia and is taught in all schools. In most of the secondary schools, it is the main language of instruction.

The official religion in Ethiopia is Christian Coptic, which has been the source of national culture and a major catalyst of all national feeling for 1,600 years. The first Bishop of Aksum was consecrated by Athanasius, Patriarch of Alexandria. The Coptic Church of Ethiopia perpetuates the liturgy it obtained from Alexandria and preaches the doctrine of the single nature of God. The Ethiopian bishop was traditionally selected from Alexandria until 1948 when the Emperor secured a concession from the Patriarch of Alexandria allowing the Ethiopian Church to select its own bishop. Coptic Christians number slightly more than half of the total population. The next largest group are the Moslems who comprise about 40 per cent of the population. Catholic and Protestant churches have only a small number of adherents, totaling less than a hundred thousand or less than 1 per cent of the population.

An atmosphere of international romance has surrounded much of Ethiopia's history. The Queen of Sheba in Biblical times was a visitor of King Solomon, and during the Middle Ages, Europe was full of stories about Prester John, the Christian monarch of Ethiopia.

Ethiopia's history antedates Christianity. Historians believe that a group of colonists of the Semitic Sabaean civilization from the Arabian peninsula settled on the Red Sea coast. The colonists, mostly merchants and traders, had contacts with ancient Egypt, Greece and Asia Minor and maintained close ties with the Arab homeland. By the end of the first century A.D., there was the equivalent of an organized state centered around Aksum. Little is known about the Aksumite kingdom which flourished for six centuries from the first to the seventh century. The architectural ruins of the kingdom near the Ethiopian-Eritrean border tell the story of an advanced civilization whose power and influence once spread across the Red Sea into the country of their ancestors.

King Aezanas, fourth century Christian ruler of Aksum, led the Ethiopian struggle against the Nubians. During this period Aksum fell under the spiritual influence of Alexandria and established the religious communion with the Coptic Church of Egypt which has persisted to this day.

During the Middle Ages, rumors prevalent in Europe about the Christian kingdom of Prester John in East Africa were of particular interest to the Portuguese who were extending their control around the African coast and to India. A Portuguese alliance with the Ethiopians would protect this shipping line to India and assist in future military activities against the Sultan of Cairo by opening up for attack his Egyptian dependencies in the rear and at the same time bar entry to the Red Sea through which the spices, gold and precious merchandise of the Orient passed.

After several unsuccessful but adventurous attempts to establish contact with the Christian kingdom of East Africa, a Portuguese envoy in 1520 did establish contact with Prester John and his Ethiopian court. This was a noteworthy event as it marked Ethiopia's public reentry into the Western world. It was also fortunate for Ethiopia that the contact with the Western world was reestablished at this time. This period was the eve of the most ferocious of the Moslem invasions. Although Portuguese aid was modest, when it did arrive in 1543 it helped to stave off the tide of Moslem conquest.

This difficult period in Ethiopian history was to be quickly followed by warfare with pagan tribes of the south and religious problems created by the attempts of the Jesuits to bring the conservative and tenacious Ethiopians into communion with the Roman Catholic Church.

The period between the departure of the Portuguese in 1633 and the mid-nineteenth century was fraught with chaos, internecine feuds and conspiracies. The traditional symbol of leadership in Ethiopia—the monarchy—fell into eclipse and decline. The confusion and bitterness of religious rebellion and civil war and the ceaseless pressure and penetration of the Galla tribes contributed to a decline. The remarkable fact is that during the period of degeneration the faith and institutions of the country still retained their traditional form. Furthermore, able rulers who held control from time to time aroused the loyalty of the people, maintained a fair degree of order and waged effective war with their enemies.

It was not until the mid-nineteenth century that the monarchy reasserted itself sufficiently to give a sense of national direction to the Ethiopian people. Although Emperor Theodore was eccentric, his contradictory nature embraced both liberal and reactionary ideas. He brought in foreign advisers for his government, mostly English. A subsequent difficulty with the English precipitated his suicide in 1868. By 1872, when John IV of Aksum secured the crown, the European grab for African colonies shattered forever Ethiopia's seclusion beyond the Simen ranges.

Imperialist designs on Ethiopia were being developed by various European powers when Menelik became emperor in 1889. The Italians were to commit the first overt aggressive act. In one of the greatest military victories won by an African country, Menelik defeated the Italians at Aduwa in 1896. This battle was one of the most decisive in Ethiopia's history. It clearly showed the world that the Ethiopians would not be parceled out to the highest bidder. The victory for Menelik is important for other reasons. It marked the beginning of a half century of progress during which the country made great strides, especially in her relations with the other nations of the world. The fifty-year period of great advances made possible by Menelik's victory at Aduwa assured Ethiopia of sufficient time to be fully accepted as a nation. When she was subsequently annexed by the Italians in 1936, Ethiopia was regarded as a nation with every claim to emancipation when the drama of international destiny would make this possible.

Menelik's reign marked the emergence of Ethiopia as a modern state concerned with the best interests of its people. It was under his leadership that the present capital, Addis Ababa (New Flower), was built.

The last four years of Menelik's reign, from 1909 to 1913, found him, because of illness and age, unable to maintain his vigorous leadership. When he died in 1913 rivalries were already formed. Three leaders emerged upon the death of Menelik as power centers: the Empress Zauditu, daughter of Menelik; Fitaurari Habta Giorghis, a prominent general; and Ras (Prince) Tafari Makonnen, son of Menelik's chief adviser. The empress and the Ras Tafari were opposite leadership types. The empress was conservative and distrustful of international contact while Ras Tafari was liberal, interested in the advancement of his people and an internationalist. When Habta Giorghis died in 1926 Ras Tafari consolidated his forces. In 1930, shortly after the empress died, he claimed title and was crowned His Imperial Majesty Haile Selassie I.

### The Emperor's Early Life

Haile Selassie stands today as a descendent of the oldest and longest line of royalty in recorded history and the reigning monarch of one of the oldest Christian nations in the world. The emperor is reputed to be the 255th monarch of the line founded by the union of King Solomon and the Queen of Sheba. Haile Selassie is unquestionably the center of political and spiritual power in Ethiopia.

The emperor was born on July 23, 1892, in Harar Province. Before he took the royal name of Haile Selassie, meaning the "instrument in power of the Trinity," he was known as Ras Tafari. His father, Ras Makonnen, was the brilliant and trusted lieutenant of Emperor Menelik. The future emperor's life has been

peculiarly fated to endure hardship and sorrow. Ten brothers and
sisters died in childhood in a boating accident on Lake Aramaya
and Ras Tafari was the only one of the eleven saved from drown-
ing. Later he spent seven years in Europe, and learned French
in a mission school. When he was fifteen his father died, in 1907,
and shortly afterward his guardian, Ras Tassama, was poisoned.
At the time of his father's death, Ras Tafari had returned to
Addis Ababa to resume his studies. As a young man concerned
with his responsibilities as a nobleman, he accepted the appointment of governor of Sidamo at the age of eighteen. In 1910 he
became governor of Harar and subsequently Muleta and Salali.

The emperor has been known for his devotion to his family.
On July 30, 1911, he married Waizero Menan, granddaughter of
King Mikhail of Wollo. In his family life, as in his early youth,
there has been sorrow. Of the imperial couple's six children, only
two sons and a daughter are living. The recent death of Sahli
Selassie, the Duke of Harar, is one of the recent tragedies in the
emperor's life.

Ras Tafari's ascension to the throne was full of exciting events.
After Emperor Menelik's death, the grandson of Menelik, Lij
Yasu, became emperor. But by 1916 the Shoan chiefs rebelled
against his misrule and his support of the Germans, Turks and
the Moslems. Lij Yasu's efforts to create a federation of Moslem
states precipitated his excommunication as head of the Ethiopian
Church in 1916. Ras Tafari was able to rally the chiefs, now re-
lieved of their oaths of fealty, and with the aid of the Allies, Yasu
and his father, Michael, were defeated at Sagalle on October 27,
1916. When he was only twenty-one, Ras Tafari was named Heir
to the Imperial Throne and Regent at the side of Empress
Zauditu. Former Emperor Lij Yasu was held by the followers of
Ras Kassa who had agreed with the Shoan chiefs not to deliver
him to Ras Tafari. This was a compromise to prevent anyone from
becoming strong enough to seize the government.

Empress Zauditu reigned for twelve years. She was a rallying point for reaction and was uninterested in enforcing any central governmental arrangement in Ethiopia. As a result, three rivals confronted Ras Tafari as opponents to his authority: Ras Hailu, governor of Gojjam; Dejazmach Balcha, ruler of the province of Sidamo; Ras Gugsa, governor of the province of Begemeder and husband of the empress. Ras Hailu wanted local supremacy for each tribe and province without any interference from the central government. Ras Gugsa was openly contemptuous of central government, and the Dejazmach was himself independently powerful. These were three great forces opposed to Ras Tafari.

In 1924 the future emperor went to Europe. There he won friends and absorbed culture and techniques that he would subsequently use to modernize Ethiopia. When he returned he found that the empress had allowed herself to become involved in a variety of palace intrigues. In a series of skillfully managed maneuvers, the prince regent managed to neutralize the various dissident groups and obtained full control over public affairs. He was crowned on November 2, 1930, as Haile Selassie I, King of Kings, Conquering Lion of Judea and Elect of God.

Now began a series of quick changes. In the first year of his reign he decreed a constitution and a parliament, an independent judicial system and central administrative departments. He then embarked upon a systematic program of building Ethiopia into a modern state. One of his great problems was that the traditional concept of leadership in Ethiopia was personalized in the ruler, who by tradition ruled through divine right. Despite this, the emperor's clear policy was to centralize and modernize the government under the Crown and to raise Ethiopia's status among the world community of nations. He immediately gave special attention to the development of health services and a broader educational system. Unfortunately, he had very little time to bring all these good things about for his people. In October, 1934, in complete violation of her treaties and numerous public statements, Italy embarked upon an aggressive war against Ethiopia.

### His Greatest Test

Italian interest in Ethiopia began with Italy's first colonies purchased in March, 1870, from a local sultan at Assab. Italy deliberately expanded and consolidated her coastal holdings until an anxious King John sought to halt the movement with war. In 1889 he died from a stray bullet and Menelik II negotiated the Uccialli Treaty with Italy. War broke out in 1895 between Italy and Ethiopia. These hostilities proved to be disastrous for Italy. The Ethiopians defeated the Italians at Aduwa in 1896, a decisive battle which gave them the distinction of being the only African people who had decisively defeated a European power in the nineteenth-century European grab for Africa.

When Emperor Menelik died in 1913 the country was plunged into international intrigues. France, England and Italy had increased their commercial activities during Menelik's reign but as the emperor's stabilizing influence waned and vanished an Anglo-French-Italian agreement was signed in 1906. Under this agreement (without consulting Ethiopia) these powers agreed to maintain the status quo but should it be disturbed, the powers were to take whatever steps necessary to safeguard their own interests in Ethiopia. The period of weakened leadership in Ethiopia which occurred under Lij Yasu's reign, fortunately coincided with the World War I period when European powers had neither the time nor energy to devote to extraterritorial interests in Ethiopia.

After World War I Ethiopia was still fearful of the 1906 Anglo-French-Italian understanding. In 1923, under Haile Selassie's careful guidance, Ethiopia was admitted to the League of Nations. Now the Ethiopians felt that they had some protection from the European powers.

During the 1920's Mussolini's designs on Ethiopia became apparent. He made no secret of the fact that he thought that restoration of Italy's national self-confidence demanded colonial conquest. He sought to wipe out the humiliating memory of the

Italian defeat at Aduwa. Mussolini preached the glories of war as a pillar of national strength and as a way of relieving, through conquest, the congested population in Italy. All the time reaffirming his peaceful intentions in Africa, Mussolini placed his most experienced colonial commander, Graziani, as Governor of Somalia, and General Emilio de Bono as High Commissioner of Eritrea.

Having judged the gamble he was making, Mussolini called a huge mass meeting of his supporters for October 2, 1935. Shouting from his balcony to a wildly cheering crowd and with his words carried by radio across the world and heard on two nationwide American radio networks, Il Duce denounced the Ethiopians.

I refuse to believe that the authentic people of Britain will want to spill blood and send Europe to its catastrophe for the sake of a barbarian country unworthy of ranking among civilized nations. . . . Italy of the Black Shirt Revolution, rise to your feet, let the cry of your determination rise to the skies and reach our soldiers in East Africa. . . .

Already, the presumably nonbarbarian Italian planes were bombing the virtually defenseless people of Ethiopia.

Although Haile Selassie, calling upon the tremendous patriotism of his people, put over a million men in the field to defend their homeland, they were no match for the mechanized army of Italy. The New York *Times* declared it was "as if a military juggernaut of the twentieth century were seeking to annihilate an army arising miraculously out of a page of ancient history. On Ethiopian soil the military world of 1935 and that of centuries ago are at grips." The *Times* estimated the Italian forces at 250,000 and the Ethiopian at a million; but the latter could effectively deploy only about the same number as the Italians in any one place and had to contend against airplanes, tanks and poison gas—the weapons of what Mussolini implied was a highly civilized country.

Ironically, the nations of the League which failed to implement effective sanctions were themselves the victim of an equally unprovoked attack within three years. Seen in retrospect, Ethiopia was forced to play the same tragic role for Italy that Spain did for the Nazis and the Communists.

When the Fascist legions crossed the border at Tigre and began the aggressive assault on Ethiopia, the emperor sent forth a unifying call for support to defend the homeland.

"It is better to die free than to live as slaves," he declared. The Ethiopians fought bravely and heroically but by the spring of 1936, the Italians forced the emperor and a small coterie of followers to flee the country. He proceeded immediately to Geneva where, in one of the historic addresses of the twentieth century, he called upon the conscience of mankind "to recognize the justice which is due to my people." In his address the emperor warned that if his small country could be treated in such a shameful way, other countries were also in danger. How right he was!

In the hushed halls of the League of Nations at Geneva on June 29, 1936, when the serene emperor of Ethiopia began to deliver his thunderous challenge to the conscience of the world, those present heard not only a challenge but an eloquent defense of the doctrine of collective security. In his opening remarks he said

There is no precedent for a head of state himself speaking in this Assembly. But there is also no precedent for a people being victim of such injustice and being at present threatened by abandonment to its aggressor. Also, there has never before been an example of any government proceeding to the systematic extermination of a nation by a barbarous means, in violation of the most solemn promises made to all the nations of the earth that there should be no resort to a war of conquest, and that there should not be used against innocent human beings the terrible poison of harmful gases.

The Ethiopian leader clearly enunciated the atrocities committed against his people by declaring

The very refinement of barbarism consisted in carrying ravage and terror into the most densely populated parts of the territory—the points farthest removed from the scene of hostilities. The object was to scatter fear and death over a great part of the Ethiopian territory. These fearful tactics succeeded. Men and animals succumbed. The deadly rain that fell from the aircraft made all those whom it touched fly shrieking with pain. All those who drank the poisoned water or ate the infected food also succumbed in dreadful suffering. In tens of thousands the victims of the Italian mustard gas fell. It is in order to denounce to the civilized world the tortures inflicted upon the Ethiopian people that I resolved to come to Geneva.

With the ambitious plans of Hitler and Mussolini already revealed, the emperor's words began to suggest what would happen to other small nations if the aggression against his people went unchallenged. All too accurately he revealed the fatal impotence of the League.

What real assistance was given to Ethiopia by the fifty-two nations who had undertaken to prevent the triumph of the aggressor? Has each of the member states, as was its duty to do in virtue of its signature appended to Article XVI of the Covenant, considered the aggressor as having committed an act of war personally directed against itself? I had placed all my hopes in the execution of these undertakings. My confidence had been confirmed by the repeated declarations made in the Council to the effect that aggression must not be rewarded and that force would be compelled to bow before right. . . . In vain!

In the quiet stillness that comes when men hear truth but do not have the courage to answer, the lone voice went on to say:

I assert that the problem submitted to the Assembly today is a much wider one. It is not merely a question of the settlement of Italian aggression. It is collective security; it is the very existence of the League of Nations. It is the confidence that each state is to place in international treaties. It is the value of promises made to small states that their integrity and independence shall be respected and ensured. It is the principle of the equality of states on the one hand, or otherwise the obligation laid down upon small powers to accept the bonds of vassalship. In a word, it is international morality that is at stake.

Thus did Haile Selassie signal the effective end of the League of Nations as a force in world affairs.

In that sad year of 1936 the world's leaders did not have the courage to accept the challenge given to them by the courageous Ethiopian leader—to prove dramatically to dictators that the nations of the free world would stick together and preserve the rights of all nations in accordance with the collective security doctrine of the League of Nations. The League chose to ignore the Italian aggression which had been committed in violation of international treaties. Disillusioned by this lack of moral integrity and shocked further by the fact that many of these same nations within a few years recognized Italy's conquest, the Emperor declared, "Never shall I cease to hope—I still have faith in the ultimate triumph of international justice."

Eventually he made his home in England where he lived as a modest and lonely hero. His days there, however, were not idle ones. The emperor became a familiar figure in Parliament, pressing his case. His persistence was rewarded when England entered the war against the Axis. Assured of British assistance, he went as a civilian to Alexandria, there to plan and prepare for his reentry into Ethiopia. Using Khartoum as a staging area, he rallied his scattered forces who, after strenuous months of training, marched with him toward the Ethiopian border. Now supported by renewed oaths of allegiance from most of his chiefs, the emperor entered Ethiopia on January 15, 1941. On May 5, 1941, exactly five years after occupation forces had taken over Addis Ababa, His Imperial Majesty reentered his capital at the head of his resistance forces who, with British troops, had fought their way into Ethiopia from the Sudan.

Always a deeply religious man, the first act of the emperor was to enter the cathedral in his capital where, quietly and alone, he thanked God for having delivered his people from their unjust oppression. Shortly after this, in one of his first official proclamations, he called upon the Ethiopian people to follow Christian principles and forego acts of revenge against the sixty thousand Italians trapped by the Ethiopian liberation forces. And in one of the great collective acts of Christian charity, the Ethiopian people, despite the black record of Fascist warfare and occupation, followed the advice of their emperor and committed no major atrocities or acts of violence against the Italians.

After restoring independence, the emperor embarked upon the prodigious job of reorganizing his country and establishing effective governmental control. Most of his capable and educated young men had been killed in the war. There were few to take their places. His financial resources were depleted. In spite of these difficulties, the emperor had, by 1945, firmly established supremacy of the central government.

## New Stature as International Leader

In the summer of 1950 the emperor simply set forth his three-point program: for the expansion of education, improvement of communications and development of more opportunities for employment.

In 1930, when he became emperor, there had been less than ten schools. By 1935 he had laid the foundation for a system of state schools to relieve the burden of the church. By 1954 there were ten thousand elementary church schools and 416 state schools, twenty-four secondary schools and ten schools of higher education. Over 10 per cent of the national budget is allocated for educational purposes. The Haile Selassie I University offers liberal arts, law and science. Nearly one thousand Ethiopian students continue their education abroad every year.

When the emperor was crowned, Ethiopia had less in the way of communications than the average American city. Today she has a profitable airline which reaches twenty-three cities within the nation and connects with international services at seven foreign airfields. An expanding postal system, four thousand miles of telegraph line and three thousand miles of all-weather roads also represent his efforts. Radio has speeded up communications within the country and provides connections with international radio-telegraphic services. Although there are two rail lines, most of the surface hauling is done by trucks and buses. One of the two railroads, the Franco-Ethiopian Line, is 486 miles long and connects Addis Ababa with the French Somaliland port of Djibouti. The second has 207 miles of track in Eritrea. In addition to its three thousand miles of all-weather roads, the empire has four thousand miles of roads that are open and passable except during the rainy seasons. Transportation in the remote areas of the interior is by mule, donkey and camel over about fifty-two hundred miles of trails and dirt roads.

Employment for every Ethiopian, the third ambition of the emperor, is a problem whose solution is less difficult than for some of Ethiopia's African neighbors. The country is blessed with well watered highlands, fertile soil and a year-round growing season. The empire is potentially one of the greatest coffee, meat and grain producing areas in Africa and exports of these items are making possible the rapid economic expansion of the empire. Mineral reserves are as yet uncertain. To develop these potentials Ethiopia's government is seeking private capital in the world's financial market and has adopted basic legislation and specific regulation which provide a healthy climate for investment. The country also has great possibilities for tourism.

### Ethiopians in Korea

In spite of his disappointment with the League, the emperor gave his ardent support to the United Nations. Ethiopian troops were among the first to answer the United Nations call for troops in Korea in 1950. In his address to the Ethiopian battalion he enunciated Ethiopia's belief in the concept of collective security. He recalled that the League of Nations did not support Ethiopia in 1936 but that now, fourteen years later, Ethiopia would answer the call to help defend another small nation—Korea—against aggression. He called upon the Ethiopian soldiers to fight bravely for the cause of international morality. The records of the Korean War indicate that the Ethiopian soldiers, thousands of miles away from home, fought bravely in defense of freedom for another small country. They demonstrated that they stood foursquare behind their emperor who had declared that the principle of collective security was a fundamental doctrine.

We must recognize, then, that every nation that fights, as we have done, for the defense and maintenance of its independence has the right to expect the honor and indeed the assistance of all freedom-loving peoples.

You are departing on a long crusade in defense of that very principle for which we have so long sought—freedom and respect for the freedom of others. With such traditions and after such sacrifices, Ethiopia would be the very first nation to recognize the imperative urgency of that call of duty towards a sister nation.

It is in yet a larger sense. . . . You are defending the most sacred principle of modern international policy, that principle of collective security with which the name of Ethiopia is imperishably associated. . . .

Small nations who must so vigilantly defend their independence should regard collective security as a cornerstone of their very existence.

As he spoke to the departing troops, the emperor could not help but recall that fifteen years previous to that very month, when Ethiopia had called on the League of Nations to carry out its pledge of assisting its fellow members against aggression, there had been no assistance for Ethiopia. The nation that was deserted by its friends at the time of its greatest need was one of the first nations of the world to respond to the universal call of collective security in the Korean War.

One of the most vexing international problems facing the emperor during the past few years has been the border disputes with Somalia. This country, formerly under Italian domination and later UN trusteeship control even before it became independent in 1960, has claimed some of the Moslem areas in the Ogaden part of Ethiopia. The United Nations is presently trying to arbitrate a settlement.

In 1956–1957 Ethiopia had difficulties with Egypt over the question of Egyptian agents working with the Moslem minority in Ethiopia. However, as a result of a recent visit of the emperor to Cairo there has been some improvement in Ethiopian-Egyptian relations.

### Eritrea Restored

One of the great international accomplishments by the emperor as far as the Ethiopian people are concerned is the restoration of Eritrea to the empire. Following the war, Ethiopia made energetic claims for Eritrea. Like the former German colonies, however, Eritrea was placed under the supervision of the United Nations Trusteeship Council. Among other reasons, Ethiopia claimed Eritrea because of the territory's historical association with Ethiopia. Most Ethiopians felt that Eritrea traditionally was part of the Ethiopian Empire. On September 15, 1952, the emperor ratified a new constitution uniting Eritrea with Ethiopia. Eritrea has full power internally and Ethiopia maintains its jurisdiction over foreign affairs, defense, currency, finance, trade and communications. By this agreement, Ethiopia regains access to the sea long denied her by the annexations of England, Italy and France.

In 1955 at Bandung the Ethiopian delegation played a relatively quiet role. But at the Accra conference in 1958 the Ethiopians tooted the anticolonial horn and participated with the other African delegations enthusiastically. In a recent announcement the emperor declared, "The peoples and territories of Africa can no longer be regarded as the preserves of colonial interests and continued objects of imperial designs." He called for implementation of the self-determination doctrine when he declared, "We hope that all colonial and trusteeship territories of Africa will in the near future be called upon to decide freely as to their own destinies. The striving of the peoples of Africa to this end should serve to advance the cause of freedom and world peace in other parts of the world." In June, 1960, the emperor was host to a conference of independent African states in Addis Ababa.

In the summer of 1959 the emperor, realizing that he must look for aid wherever it could be obtained, embarked upon state visits to the United Arab Republic, the Soviet Union, Czechoslovakia, Belgium, France, Portugal and Yugoslavia. Shortly after he returned he set forth in a national address a basic economic development program. At the beginning of his reign in the early thirties he had embarked upon the immense task of modernizing a feudal country. Soon he was leading his people in defense of their freedom and continued to fight although in exile. He took the Ethiopian cause to the League of Nations and to the capitals of the world. A few years later he had freed his people from foreign occupation; now in 1959 he called upon them to work as never before for their own economic and social development. He declared:

The next step for each Ethiopian . . . is to devote himself assiduously to the execution of our plan for the betterment of our country. If we fail to use profitably the credit which we have acquired for the development of our communications system, port facilities and the establishment of industries, we shall have brought a heavy liability, not only upon ourselves but upon succeeding generations.

The forward march of the emperor calls for rapid social and economic development within the framework of Ethiopia's traditions. It is here, of course, that skeptics begin to raise their questions. Can the man who led his people in peace and war now lead them toward great strides in social and economic development? And can this development be carried out within the framework of Ethiopia's traditions? It is a problem that faces all the leaders of Black Africa today.

### The Road Ahead

The road ahead for the emperor is deeply interwoven with the nature of his country. Ethiopia is still a fascinating mixture of the old and the new. Many of its problems are the problems of most of Africa. More than 90 per cent of the population lives by traditional subsistance agriculture and has limited or no contact with the small but expanding market economy. At the same time, there are rapidly growing cities and towns with paved and lighted streets, modern shops, office buildings and hospitals. Small factories and workshops are beginning to appear on the outskirts. In the remoter countryside, Ethiopian tribesmen who had never seen a wagon, much less a train or an automobile, have accepted the scheduled planes of the Ethiopian Airlines as an ordinary event. While the overwhelming majority of the population lacks a modern type of education, the students at the new university college in Addis Ababa have courses and receive degrees equivalent to those of universities in the United States.

In the first thirty years of his reign, His Imperial Majesty has unified his people, brought them into the contemporary community of nations, electrified the world by the heroic defense of Ethiopia against the Fascist onslaught, brought independence back to his people and now is engaged in the herculean task of establishing a basis for social and economic progress.

A key problem facing the emperor in the days ahead is to reach his cherished goal of economic progress without endangering his equally beloved goal of preserving the traditional aspects of Ethiopian culture.

There are also some questions about succession that could be troublesome. Although the constitution provides for the emperor's elder son, the crown prince, to succeed him, some observers wonder if the great glory and prestige of Africa's elder statesman can really be passed on to anyone. Of course, this is the problem of any monarchy that produces an outstanding ruler.

In many ways, Ethiopia is a land that typifies reconciliation for the rest of the world. An experience I had with one of my Ethiopian classes illustrates this simply. Upon saying goodbye to the students before returning to the United States, one of the boys waited quietly until all the others had left. He came up to me and suddenly removed from his neck an Ethiopian-style cross and held it out to me as a gift. When I tried to refuse it, he insisted. His cross, he said, was also my cross. If all white and Negro peoples would recognize the same cross we would come closer to peace on earth. I accepted his gift with deep appreciation.

Ethiopia is the Christian beacon on the African continent. Despite centuries of oppression, these valiant people never bowed their heads to their oppressors. In their humble, thatch-covered chapels, the Ethiopian Christians remained faithful to their beliefs.

The road ahead for the Lion of Judah and his people might bring unexpected and difficult challenges. Yet their history tells us never to doubt the high ideals of Haile Selassie and his people —or their courage.

# IV

# Tom Mboya—
# The Young Man from Kenya

In 1950, several months after Tom Mboya had joined the staff of an agricultural research laboratory, he was alone in his agricultural station. His European superior being absent on vacation, Tom was left in charge. A European woman, wishing a dairy license, brought in a sample of milk for inspection. Looking around for several minutes, she finally asked in a very cold manner, "Is there nobody here?" While Tom controlled his anger, he never forgot the implication that he, because he was an African, was professionally incompetent and not a person with whom a European wished to deal. The hurt is made more memorable by the fact that nine years later, when I discussed Kenya with him in his New York hotel suite, he had become an acknowledged leader not only of his countrymen in Kenya but recognized by the African people generally. In 1960 at the historic Kenya Constitutional Conference in London, Tom Mboya played a leading role in directing the strategy which set the stage for changing Kenya from a European colony to an African country.

## Kenya—Land of Many Legends

Tom Mboya, like the other African leaders, is very much a product of his own country. Kenya may be divided into four geographical sections: the coastal plain rising from the Indian

Ocean on the east; the broad plateau; the eastern Rift Valley; the bordering mountains and the Lake Plateau beyond the Rift to Lake Victoria and the Uganda border. The coastal plain is narrow and to the north vegetated with scrub. Around the seacoast city of Mombasa, the climate is hot and wet. The countryside is fertile. Rising steadily, the broad, arid plateau stretches to the Ethiopian border. This plateau accounts for nearly three-fourths of Kenya, but it is too dry to support a permanent population.

Kenya's population is made up of four main races: African, approximately 6,000,000; Asian, approximately 150,000; around 33,000 Arabs and a little less than 50,000 Europeans. The Arabs are found mostly on the coastal plain, the Indians in the cities. The Africans come of several different stocks, most of whom arrived in the country from the north or northeast between the fourteenth and nineteenth centuries. It is fairly certain that the first wave was the Bantu invasion about the fourteenth century, down to the coast, up the Tana River and fanning out around Mount Kenya.

The greater part of Kenya's population lives in the well watered highlands in the center of which rises Mt. Kenya 17,058 feet. Much of the country's 220,000 square miles is too arid for anything but a nomadic existence. The highlands are one of the most densely populated parts of East Africa. This section and the southwestern part of the country are over 5,000 feet above sea level and escape the violent seasonal fluctuations common to Africa. The climate is cool but with considerable daily range in temperature.

One of the most distinctive geological features of East Africa, the Great Rift Valley, runs along the eastern edge of the highlands. It goes north to Lake Rudolf and there swings east from Ethiopia. Its immense parallel fissures slip some 2,000 feet below the plain. Its floor, rather than being flat, is dotted with volcanic cones. On the far or west side of the Rift highlands, the land runs steeply down to Lake Victoria.

Farming is restricted to the highlands. There the soil is fertile and black. Plantation crops are sisal, coffee, tea, some cereals and pyrethrum. Cattle, sheep and goats have always been raised with success and fruit is of growing importance. Maize, however, is a basic food for the African.

Pre-nineteenth century history is mostly a record of Arabs and Europeans visiting the coastal area of Kenya. Their arrivals coincided with the winds of the monsoon. These winds blew from the northwest in December and from the southwest in March. Such an arrangement helped the Arabs, Phoenicians, Hindus and possibly the Jews and Assyrians to sail across the Indian Ocean. There is also clear evidence that Chinese merchants touched African shores and it is quite possible that Egyptians traded south as early as 5000 B.C. For centuries, these visitors came for spices, ivory and slaves.

The religious leadership of Mohammed unified the various Arab tribes in this area. Following his death in A.D. 632 various defeated parties in the dispute over a rightful successor took refuge in East Africa. They came from Oman, Yemen, Persia and Mesopotamia and eventually established themselves as wealthy and successful traders along the coast. From 975 to 1498 the Zenj Empire, a series of city states, flourished.

The entry of Vasco da Gama in Malindi in 1498 marked the beginning of Portuguese control throughout the Indian Ocean. For over two centuries, his successors monopolized the eastern trade but their resources were too small to maintain their wide empire and the Arabs regained most of their old possessions by 1740. Arab control was undisputed until the French, English and Germans began biting off sections of Africa in the nineteenth century. This scramble was in many ways personified at that time by young Karl Peters of the recently unified Germany who made a vigorous bid for extensive holdings in East Africa.

From 1877 to 1890 the Germans and the British, with occasional competition from the French and Belgians, engaged in a seesaw struggle for this part of East Africa. By 1890, in spite of successful German cultivation, Germany abandoned claims to the area now called Uganda and the boundary between Kenya and Tanganyika was set. This brought the struggle for East African territory to an uneasy equilibrium.

The Brussels Conference of 1889–1890 was significant for Kenya. As a repressive measure against slavery, the conference suggested that railroads and roads be built not only to mobilize military forces but primarily to eliminate the slave caravans. Railroads would carry the trade but not the slaves. Furthermore, railroads would also ease the administration of interior Kenya and by effective occupation to Lake Victoria, England could control the headwaters of the Nile. Thus, in spite of enormous expense, the Kenya-Uganda Railroad was built. It was essentially this road that permitted the English to occupy Kenya completely.

Although Indian traders had lived along the coast for centuries, the main influx of Indians were those imported to build the railroad. In order to pay for it, the government encouraged settlers to develop the natural resources. The first Europeans to settle were dislocated persons from South Africa, refugees because of the war. However, as the fame of Kenya's climate developed, the number of Europeans increased until now the white population numbers around 50,000. The background of some of the present-day irritations in Kenya over land goes back to that period. At the turn of the century the native population had been greatly diminished by smallpox and their crops and herds had been destroyed by rinderpest, drought and locusts. In many areas the land was empty. Different concepts of ownership led to great misunderstanding over land agreements. The government first established the Masai Reserve in 1904 but only after further disagreements were the boundaries of all reserves finally settled in 1932 by the Carter Commission. Under this plan 52,097 square miles were designated for native use; 16,173 square miles for Europeans. Most observers pointed out at that time that a great deal of the native reserve was inferior land. The decision effectively to occupy Kenya was taken by the British government and not by pioneer individuals. That is, the government preceded the settlers, hence initially all political power was in the Crown. The history of Kenya is the history of the various communal groups: the European, the Indian, the African, striving to wrest this power from the Crown for themselves; in effect, organizing to control the government. Before 1900 the government had no plans to develop the territory and there was no real effort to encourage settlers. The Kenya-Uganda Railroad was instrumental in attracting settlers and spurring the government to encourage settlers so that the railroad would pay.

In 1903 Lord Delemere proved to the world that Europeans could make a living in Kenya and by 1905 over one million acres had been sold by the government to white settlers. A few years later he organized his European compatriots into the Colonists Association, demanding their share in the government. In 1907 the first nominated legislative council was created in repsonse to the settlers' demands. The Indians were the only other group at that time to offer any competition to the settlers. They too wanted a share of government power as well as land from the settler highlands. World War I interrupted political controversy between the groups and the government but after 1918 the settlers won their first elected representatives to the legislative council. The Indians had to be content with only nominated representatives and the stated government policy of placing European interests first was paramount.

Arguments between these two groups over representation, discrimination and land precipitated a government "White Paper" declaring African interests paramount and inaugurating the communal role for Europeans, Indians and Arabs with Europeans still in the majority. This was in 1923. Here is a paradox then, of African paramountcy and European domination with the other communal groups squeezed from any influential position. Having been refused satisfaction the Indian group boycotted the Legislative Council. Lack of organization and internal schisms between Hindu and Moslem hampered their effectiveness but they were backstopped in their demands by India. The Indians did not re-enter the Council until 1931, and even then their grievances remained.

During the 1930's British governmental policy established the idea of trusteeship toward the Africans although still trying to accommodate the Europeans. In the meantime, the settler population was increasing through immigration. Indian immigration had been restricted by the government under settler insistence. Living habits were fast changing from rural to urban. During this time the Europeans still managed the government to the exclusion of all other groups.

The Second World War added momentum to political events. By 1944 the first African was represented on the Legislative Council. That same year the Kenya-Africa Union was established. Initially it tried to be an all-African movement but really this was a Kikuyu organization. The Kikuyu had not only the longest contact with the Europeans but also the most grievances. They lived in overcrowded areas, often in severe economic distress; they resented the lack of opportunity, the unequal wages and the unequal distribution of land. Under Jomo Kenyatta, the Kenya-Africa Union demanded that Africans be allowed to own land anywhere, that European settlement be halted, that Africans be settled in the unused parts of the highlands, that Africans be given the franchise in equal representation on the Legislative Council. In 1950 the KAU, by now a completely nationalistic organization, went underground, having been outlawed by the government. In 1952 the horror of Mau Mau erupted.

That year, 1952, is an important date in recent Kenya history. By then there had been significant constitutional changes—increased African participation on the Legislative Council, the achievement of an unofficial majority although European-controlled, a reorganization of the ministerial system to include non-Europeans and the establishment of the East African High Commission with jurisdiction over transportation and communications between Kenya, Tanganyika and Uganda. But in spite of some concessions the Europeans still felt they should completely control the government and that any African movement to do so was subversive. Most independent observers feel that the KAU was a cover for Mau Mau although some executive members were not involved and Mau Mau had little success in non-Kikuyu areas.

### Tom Mboya—Leadership Opportunity at an Early Age

Tom Mboya belonged to the KAU but during that organization's difficult years, 1950 to 1952, he was too young to be influential in a movement firmly controlled by Jomo Kenyatta. The vacuum of leadership that occurred as a result of the deportation and jailing of Kenyatta, the mass arrests during the Mau Mau difficulties and Tom's own organizational abilities provided a springboard which allowed him within a few years to become internationally known as an African leader.

Tom was born on a sisal estate in Kenya's white highlands on August 15, 1930. His father and mother were both illiterate but they had been converted into the Catholic Church by the missionaries who lived on the estate. As a baby (the first of six children born to his parents), Tom was baptized Thomas in the Catholic Church. According to tradition, his mother gave him the name Odhiambo signifying the time of his birth—evening. His parents gave him the second clan name of Mboya. Today, though he is better known as Tom Mboya, his mother still insists on calling him Thomas.

During Tom's early youth his father worked as a laborer for a few dollars a month, later being promoted to overseer. Although the senior Mr. Mboya did not have the opportunity for formal education, he was determined to give his children an education not only because he wanted them to have a higher standard of living, but also because this constituted a safe investment for him against old age—a general African conception of education.

His father saved his meager earnings for months to be able to pay for his oldest boy's yearly school fees. Tom first went to the Catholic mission school, Kabaa, in the Ukamba District of Kenya, in 1939. In a brief autobiographical article, Tom recalls from his early school days that, "We learned our lessons under a tree and since we had no books or slates on which to learn, we used sand. The teachers, a Catholic priest and a few Africans, shared a few blackboards between the classes. Some children walked fifteen to twenty miles to get to school."

Responsibilities came early to young Tom. When he was thirteen and still in secondary school, his younger brothers were now ready for school and his father, already overburdened with the financial responsibilities of paying school fees, needed help. Tom then began "working his way through school" by jobs after classes and during the holidays.

When in 1947 he completed high school, his grades were high enough for him to go on to advanced studies. Faced with the decision of continuing his own education or assisting his younger brothers, Tom left school and sought employment so that he could give educational opportunities to the younger members of his family.

### Early Leadership Period

In discussing his early nationalist motivations with me, the Kenya leader said that his school years were influential in directing his ambitions. While only a young boy he became aware of the grave inequalities between white and black. During his early school days, while giving all the appearances of being just another happy schoolboy, he decided on a future career of political action. An active debater, he regarded the debating society as a prime opportunity to crystallize his ideas and cultivate his political talents. It is quite apparent that he resents his past poverty and the limitations it placed upon his education.

In 1948 Tom Mboya joined the Royal Sanitary Institute Medical Training School for sanitary inspectors at Nairobi and later moved to Jeanes School, a few miles out of Nairobi. Tom was later to say, "While at Jeanes School my mind was made up as to what I should do when I came out. I had lived in poverty and squalor. I was bitter at not being able to go on to school for lack of money. I was determined I would work for the improvement of conditions of African workers and for the education of African children." Within a few months after entering the government training school, he was elected president of the student council. This was a powerful body for it made decisions on the use of school funds and other administrative matters. It was here that he had his first real experience of politics. Here also he learned to dispute and to push for his own ideas, for the principal of the school was a Kenya European with whom Tom frequently disagreed. In 1950 he qualified as a sanitary inspector and was appointed to the staff of the Nairobi City Council in 1951. In commenting on his first professional position, Tom later said, "I earned less than one-fifth of the European inspector's salary." Tom was now twenty-one, determined and dedicated. He turned to trade unionism as a means of aiding his people. He chose this medium rather than the already organized political movement for a number of reasons. As a city employee he belonged to the African Staff Association, at that time an impotent group but a natural for political organization. Furthermore, he was too young to be influential in the KAU which was firmly controlled by Kenyatta. When he joined the Kenya Africa Union he was warned that such activities would not help his career. Without any hesitation he resigned his job and devoted full time to trade union activities. In 1953 he was chosen General Secretary of the Kenya Federation of Labor, a post he still holds. The great opportunity that Tom had always hoped for—the opportunity to help large numbers of his fellow Africans—came in 1955 during the dockworkers' strike in Mombasa. Principally through his dynamic leadership and energetic organizing activities, Tom settled the strike of four thousand dockworkers and won an increase of thirty cents an hour. With this tremendous victory for the Africans, Tom's reputation spread throughout Kenya. He now had the solid backing of Kenya's labor force. It has been this power which started him on the road to African leadership.

*Spokesman for Africa*

In 1954 the Lyttelton settlement agreed in principle that Africans should be elected to the Legislature. In March, 1957, Kenya Africans voted for the first time, returning a total of eight African members. The African members immediately demanded increased representation, and that year the Lennox Boyd Constitution changed the number from eight to fourteen African elected members and two ministerial posts. It also included provision for twelve members especially elected by the Legislature to form the basis of a future nonracial qualitative franchise. This compromise was possibly only because the Europeans were allowed greater ministerial control. The additional six African members were elected in March, 1958. They declined a ministerial post and boycotted the new Lennox Boyd Constitution. When the four Africans were elected to serve as the special representatives, Mboya's group issued a strong critical statement of them. Six of Mboya's followers and himself were charged with defamation and conspiracy in a trial held in May, 1958. Mboya was convicted of criminal libel and given a small fine of seventy-five pounds.

Mboya has traveled extensively abroad, especially in Europe, the rest of Africa and the United States. The culmination of his efforts internationally was the All African Peoples Conference held in Accra in December, 1958. His election as Chairman and the fact that Dr. Kwame Nkrumah of Ghana shared the spotlight with him, brought him world attention.

He has also been active in the leadership of the anti-Communist International Confederation of Free Trade Unions. In his major address at the 1958 All African Peoples Conference in Accra, his theme was "Hands Off Africa!" and the conference followed his lead. It warned the world against all types of imperialism in Africa and established a permanent secretariat to advance the cause of African independence.

Mr. Mboya made a big hit in his 1959 tour of the United States. He was received by Vice President Nixon and other leaders. During his tour he spoke frequently on international questions. Mr. Mboya believes there is some Communist influence in some African territories.

Both poverty and illiteracy provide an opportunity for Communist operations. As long as our people live in poverty, disease and ignorance, there is danger of communism. . . . The West would be fooled into a false sense of security, if it paid all its attention to Europe and if it did not realize that Africa, even though now peaceful, will soon be the area of major world consequences. The West must realize that it cannot fight communism successfully by negative measures, shortterm plans and emergency reactions. As I see it, the West must cease waiting until the Communists strike. The West should sell international democracy just as they [the Russians] try to peddle international communism.

The young African leader does not hesitate to point out the weaknesses of the West's position. He has been particularly critical of its double standard of international morality. He feels that the West condemns the East for Hungary and Tibet but hedges on Algeria and South Africa.

These very different standards based on whether or not someone is a friend do not help the West. They lead the people of Africa and Asia to doubt the honesty of the West. It leads these nations to adopt policies of neutralism and nonalignment. They do not agree with the

East, but doubt the West. They do not always see the East-West struggle as one between communism and democracy. They see it as a power struggle between East and West, and they fear that they may be the pawns if they join either side.

In an address given on Africa Freedom Day on April 15, 1959, in New York City the young man from Kenya proposed a positive program of cooperation between the West and Africans. He said:

Let us, therefore, join together and match the internationalism of communism, item by item, with the internationalism of democracy. Let us cooperate in the effort to eliminate disease, poverty and ignorance from the face of the earth, and we shall have dealt a death blow to the root causes of most of the "isms" that currently bedevil the world.

To those who count, instead, upon military bases, established in colonial areas without consent of—or even notice to—the local inhabitants for security against the false prophets of the world, I commend a thorough study of recent events. Military agreements negotiated with colonial powers will necessarily be, as they are today in Morocco, for example, subject to the will and the needs of the African people when they gain their independence. I humbly submit that only Africans, whatever their color, background, or race, may rightfully decide matters which vitally affect the future of Africa. We African people seek the same peace, stability, security, and well-being that all decent people seek the world over, and we are unwilling to be used willy-nilly as pawns in a great power struggle. For this reason we adamantly oppose the use of any African territory, even the most desolate wastes of the Sahara, as a testing ground by non-Africans of their new and ever more devilish instruments of destruction.

In the same address Mr. Mboya had a special message for Americans when he said:

My friends, our struggle is simple. It is for political freedom, economic opportunity and human dignity for all Africans, goals which can be opposed only by those who oppose the very concepts of democracy and human rights. Our struggle for freedom will continue without compromise until the liberation of all Africa is achieved.

You are the descendents of the tiny brave band of men who "fired the shot heard around the world." Its sound has been slow to reach Africa, but now the echoes rebound from every corner of the land. For the same freedom and right to a better life which your ancestors won with so much pain and suffering, we Africans now also strive. To this achievement for every African in every portion of the continent we too pledge "our lives, our fortunes, and our sacred honor."

Fundamentally friendly to the West and to the United States, the Kenya leader has not hesitated to advise the West on what to do to prevent Africa from falling into the Soviet sphere of influence. He has said:

The West should be in countries before the Communists get there, not after. The West should put democracy into action in these countries so that there will be no opportunity for the Communists. This means that the West must face up to the problems in the underdeveloped parts of the world—with capital, with technical aid, with understanding of the emerging peoples and their problems. The West must have a long-term program of assistance to new nations in their struggle to gain independence and to overcome poverty, disease and ignorance.

Tom Mboya's greatest victory for the people of Kenya occurred in London in the winter of 1960. It is a victory that has made his name a byword not only among his fellow countrymen but throughout freedom-conscious Africa. In late January, 1960, Tom Mboya and the entire African elected membership sat down at London's Lancaster House for a round-table conference with British and Kenya government officials and white and Asian delegates. When they arrived at the conference, Kenya was a crown colony. Six weeks later Tom Mboya and his fellow African delegates left with the outline for a totally new Kenya. In general the principal terms for the new Kenya are:

1. A common voting role and liberalized voting standards that will increase the number of eligible African voters to around a million for the general elections (to be held in the spring of 1961).

2. A sixty-five-member legislature in which Africans seem sure of a clear majority of thirty-seven seats.

3. A new cabinet in which Africans are promised several ministries.

4. A bill of rights, still to be drafted, guaranteeing equality and protection of property rights, by judicial safeguards. The old system of reserve land for separate races, like the white highlands, would be swept away.

The Kenya leader sees these terms as the framework for a republic within the British Commonwealth. He would have it committed politically to neither East nor West but guided by Western principles of freedom, which have molded his own rise to leadership.

## The Future

The young man from Kenya still possesses the charm of the barefooted boy who studied under a tree and wrote his lessons in the sand. But his eyes, once filled with a young boy's twinkle, now sparkle with the realization that within his brief life he has played a significant role in bringing the long-cherished independence within the grasp of his people.

Much remains to be done. The four key provisions set forth in the Kenya Constitutional Conference at London in 1960 must be transformed into a reality in the immediate future. Furthermore, the patience that the Kenya leaders have demonstrated toward European and Asian citizens will be continually tested in the years immediately ahead. The young leader and his associates who have suffered indignities because of their color must dramatize, now that they have the political power, that the insults and indignities will be returned by African fair play.

There are some who doubt this and predict not only inequalities for non-African citizens but also harm and suffering. I for one will venture the opinion that here, in the bright, cool highlands of East Africa, the world will see still another sign that this continent can be a place of reconciliation and good will.

# V

## Julius Nyerere—
## Architect of a New Nation

When this quiet but eloquent schoolmaster left the sanctuary of his schoolroom in 1954 there was nothing to indicate that within six years Tanganyika, under his wise, dedicated but moderate leadership, would stand at the doorstep of independence. Tanganyika gained responsible self-government in late 1960, prelude to full independence within a few years, and Dr. Nyerere was named Chief Minister.

Julius Kambarage Nyerere, the former shepherd boy, is the architect of this new nation which is joining the world family of nations.

His appeal to his countrymen has been addressed to their minds and he has won their hearts by his tireless and brilliant efforts in their behalf. His own climb upward from a son of a tribal chieftain to a position alongside the leaders of the world has been an inspiration to them.

Some observers feel that Julius' personality and temperament reflect the kind of leader that the Tanganyikan people have subconsciously always wanted. The land has been free of the racial tensions and antiforeign agitation that has occurred in some other areas of Africa. Perhaps it is more than coincidental that Tanganyika, the land of snow-capped Mount Kilimanjaro and Africa's three most beautiful lakes, should have quietly brought about the great political changes that have occurred within its own boundaries during the past few years and pushed its people into the vanguard of Africans who have achieved dramatic sociopolitical improvements since the period of great change began in Africa in 1946.

## Tanganyika—Showcase for Racial Cooperation

Tanganyika has 362,688 square miles or roughly the equivalent of the United States' Southwest. Its highlands include the beautiful snow-covered Mount Kilimanjaro, over 19,000 feet high. The narrow coastal plain rises gently to the plateau which maintains an average altitude of about 4,000 feet. It is mostly flat, dry and lightly wooded. Rivers flow either to the Indian Ocean or into the lakes to the west.

The country has three climatic zones. The warm humid coast is equatorial with the temperature seldom below 80° during the two rainy seasons from October to May. The hot, dry plateau provides for considerable seasonal and daily variations in temperature with cool nights and hot days. The mean temperature is over 70°. The third climatic zone is semitemperate. This region is in the highlands to the north and the Crater Highland to the west where the altitude ranges from five to ten thousand feet.

The only extractive industry is the diamond mines. Commercial farming is hampered by the aridity and lack of communications, and the tsetse fly limits extensive animal husbandry. Although most of the agriculture is of the subsistence type, Tanganyika is the world's greatest exporter of sisal. Hides, coffee and cotton are also exported. Tobacco grows in Tanganyika and as a local industry could save valuable foreign exchange. Julius Nyerere is interested in stimulating local production of cigarettes and other tobacco products.

The population of Tanganyika is more than 9 million people, composed of about 8.9 million Africans, 25,000 Europeans, 76,-900 Indians and 19,000 Arabs. The African group includes 120 to 200 tribes with the Sukuma representing about 12 per cent of the population. There are also tribes that have strong aboriginal characteristics—the Bushman-Pygmy type—indicating their descent from the oldest tribes on the continent. Following the Negroid migrations came the Hamitic peoples from Western Asia. It was this early group that mixed with the Negroes to form the Bantu language complex. Lighter-skinned nomadic Hamites followed and in the nineteenth century there were intrusions of Masai from the north and Zulus from the south into the Tanganyika territory.

The written history of Tanganyika began with the Arab colonization. Some claim this colonization came with the spread of Islam about the eighth century A.D. but the presence of ruins indicates the possibility of earlier movements from Arabia and Persia. The oldest known town, for example, is Kilwa, founded in 975. The town was also used as a post for the Portuguese in 1505. Ruins still show a mosque, palace and fort.

These Arab colonies are believed to have reached their height between A.D. 1100 and 1300 and again in 1400. During this time there was considerable prosperity. A rather advanced civilization flourished on ivory, gold, tortoise shell, ambergris and slaves. These riches were known throughout the world and brought traders from China and mercantile Europe.

The arrival of the Portuguese in 1498 meant domination by Portugal of Tanganyika's coast as it did with Kenya. Throughout the sixteenth century the Portuguese controlled the coastal towns, ruling in conjunction with tributary Arab sultans. This arrangement lasted until 1622 when rebellious Arabs staged a series of uprisings. The coast then fell to Saif Bin Sultan, Iman of Muscat. By 1749 Portuguese influence was relegated to Mozambique and Arab influence centered in Zanzibar.

The unique feature of Tanganyika during this period was the slave trade. The Masai to the north and the Zulus to the south limited the trade by their warlike reputations. The history of the slave route in this part of Africa is one of deeper and deeper penetration into the interior. Three slave routes ran through the Tanganyika territory. There are many vivid accounts of this trade which stopped only in the late nineteenth century. The territory was then controlled by Seyyid Said (1829–1856), Sultan of Zanzibar. He established a firm check on the trade with the aid of the British. British influence was great in the Sultan's palace from 1870 to 1885.

Christian missionaries had long been active in the territory. Henry M. Stanley began his celebrated and successful expedition for James Gordon Bennett's New York *Herald* to find Dr. Livingstone in 1871, first reporting on the inauguration of the Suez Canal in 1869. Dr. David Livingstone, of course, was a Protestant missionary and on the way to find him, Stanley stopped off at a Jesuit mission, reporting enthusiastically on their hospitality.

When Dr. Karl Peters, representing the Society for German Colonization, arrived in 1884, he found the slave trade still flourishing among tribes inland and some of the caravans managed to reach the coast successfully. It was virtually the single effort of this young, vigorous but ruthless man who, by making treaties with a number of chiefs, was able to snatch Tanganyika for Germany. The agreement of 1886 shrank the Sultan's domains to a narrow coastal strip and even this he was forced to lease to the German East Africa Company. The company, formed by Peters to administer this territory, was given a charter of protection by the German government in 1885. By 1889 the Tanganyika territory was established and the border fixed.

The company wished to make radical agricultural changes by inaugurating the plantation system. It also intended to take over all the territory's trade and administrative functions. This policy precipitated Arab as well as native ire and there were uprisings from 1888 until 1907.

The company transferred administrative authority to the German government in 1891 and Peters' title was changed to Imperial High Commissioner. His reaction to the uprising was extreme cruelty. Among the natives he was known as the man with the blood-stained hands and in 1897 the government finally removed him from his post.

The German administration, handicapped by a shortage of personnel, attempted to rule the area by a form of indirect rule. In strong tribal areas chiefs maintained the rule under a German resident. In other areas Arab officials administered directly and were responsible to the commissioner. There were never over a hundred Germans to govern seven million Africans.

The development policy, however, was ambitious and eventually provoked a bloody rebellion. The government encouraged planters who in turn demanded land and labor. These demands plus a tax were greatly resented by the Africans. Violence erupted in the south in 1905 in the Maji Maji rebellion. Thousands of tribesmen bathed in a water and millet mixture which they believed made them impervious to bullets. They fought with fanatical determination, believing that their men who were killed were actually only sleeping and would rise again to fight anew. Since the Germans were unable to subdue the people by arms, they burned the crops and villages, causing famine and starvation. Through fighting and starvation it is believed a hundred and twenty thousand Africans died.

Members of the Social Democratic party and various missionary groups, shocked at this horror, insisted on administrative reforms. The government finally agreed to cease the alienation of land to the settlers and to expand communications into the highlands. Land reform, however, was minimized by settler resistance.

The country was again plunged into misery by World War I. The entire East African campaign was fought over Tanganyika bringing death from dysentery, malaria, famine and finally, the flu epidemic. It was a devastated land when the British assumed administration under the League of Nations mandate. It later became a trust territory under the United Nations.

Among other things, this means periodical visits by the UN and the submission of a yearly report to the Trusteeship Council. The territory is administered by a governor responsible to the British government. While the UN has a great deal of influence, the British government actually establishes policy for the territory.

The governor is assisted by an Executive Council and a Legislative Council. Membership in both these groups is determined by "parity," that is, equality of racial groups represented regardless of numerical differences. This policy was introduced in 1953 and at that time was unique to Tanganyika. Tanganyika has not been hamstrung by an influential European minority. The diversity of their national origins has apparently discouraged political cohesiveness among the Europeans and hence created more stability in the country.

Like all other African countries hurrying toward independence, the schools play a major role. Most of them are administered by voluntary agencies, some assisted by the government. There are, however, no facilities for higher education in the territory. As of 1956–1957 over three million pounds were allocated for education, as compared to eighty-one thousand pounds in 1935.

There are about three thousand Africans in technical, vocational and teacher-training schools and no Asians or Europeans. Since there are no institutions of higher education, around four hundred students have been receiving college training in England, Kenya and Uganda.

The mandated status of Tanganyika since 1920 was a significant factor in its political direction. As a trust territory under both the League and the UN, the assumption has always been that the peoples in this territory would eventually govern themselves. While some events may not have been in keeping with this premise, the underlying assumption of eventual independence gave a framework of reality to African political development in the territory.

### Early Days of the Leader

The most influential man, the key to recent developments in Tanganyika, is the slight, mild and boyish Julius K. Nyerere. He was born on the eastern shore of Lake Victoria, son of a chief of the Zanaki. This is a tribe of thirty to thirty-five thousand persons, many of whom herd cattle and goats. Nyerere was fortunate in being able to attend the local government schools at Masoma and Tabora for nine years and then Makerere College where he received his teaching diploma in 1946. He finished his formal education at the University of Edinburgh (1949–1952) with a master's degree in history and economics.

School was his first contact with different ideas. These ideas were crystallized at Edinburgh and during his few years of teaching. After returning to Tanganyika, the young Nyerere was a teacher at a Catholic school outside the capital of Dar es Salaam. He also entered nonpolitical groups in Dar es Salaam and there first met persons sympathetic to his plans. It seems that by this time a political organization was already in his mind and by 1953 Nyerere was the person to watch in Tanganyika. Nyerere considers himself a "troublemaker" because he believes in "human rights strongly enough to be one." A year later when his superior suggested he might have to choose between teaching and politics, Nyerere left the school to devote full time to TANU, the Tanganyika African National Union. At that time it was a small but significant organization. Now it boasts a paying membership of eight hundred thousand people. A movement springing from the people, TANU's objectives include the introduction of universal adult suffrage at both the central and local government levels, opposition to the parity system of tripartite voting, the establishment of a time table of constitutional, economic and educational development as well as the establishment of a territorial university and the increased Africanization of the public service. The party is opposed to land alienation to non-Africans and emphasizes that the territory's economy depends ultimately upon the land and labor rather than upon immigrant groups and foreign investment. The overriding and ultimate objective of TANU is the establishment of a democratic African state in which non-Africans would be guaranteed equal citizenship rights.

In the early years of TANU's life, Nyerere's only real competitor was Thomas Marealle, a self-made chief and leader of the Chagga Union. Marealle's influence was restricted to the Chagga, a virile and aggressive tribe, and also to the governor. Both he and Governor Twining harassed the new organization. But Nyerere judiciously moved forward as he is convinced that freedom can be obtained through constitutional methods.

Nyerere created a precedent for an African political leader in 1955 when he appeared before the United Nations. It was the first time an African had been sent by a territorial political organization, in this case TANU, to present his people's hopes to the UN. In his UN debut he endorsed the 1954 Visiting Missions Report recommending the establishment of a fixed date for self-government within the next twenty years. An adamant British government, however, was successful in influencing the UN not to accept the report. This occasion, however unsuccessful, gave Julius Nyerere the opportunity of communicating the aspirations of the African people to the world through the UN.

A major political problem in Tanganyika is the Indian because it is he who holds much of the wealth and power through business. Nyerere recognizes the worth of the Indian. Anyone, he says, who contributes something to the country should have a voice in the government. He insists, of course, on the preponderance of African influence but also recognizes that European know-how is essential. Already Europeans and Asians are cooperating with Mr. Nyerere.

He feels all races can live together. "TANU is going to prove
that you can have a democracy in a plural society in Africa and
have it quite happily." Many in the European community realize
their political future lies with TANU and are cooperating with
the organization. Others have joined the United Tanganyika
Party, the only group that challenged TANU in the 1958 election.

Indeed 1958 marked the introduction of an elected non-Euro-
pean in the Legislative Council. Representation was arranged by
the parity system. That is, the voter had to choose three candidates, one from each racial group. Nyerere opposed the parity
idea and in protest resigned in the spring of 1958 from his appointed seat on the Legislative Council. The government would
not consider his demand for single-member constituencies.

*Leadership Period*

However, TANU did participate in the September, 1958, elections even though parity was the basis of selection. TANU won
handily over the United Tanganyika Party and now controls the
unofficial side of the sixty-seven-member council. Since these
elections, Julius Nyerere has dominated the political scene in
Tanganyika. In September, 1960, his leadership position was confirmed with TANU's overwhelming victory at the polls.

TANU is certainly political but not agitational. Nyerere, furthermore, sees a broader purpose for the organization. It is vitally concerned with education, particularly technical education.
TANU's main objective is to prepare the people for independence. Its leader feels that education is the greatest need of a
young country.

He has also been chosen to head the Tanganyika Elected Members Organization. This is, in effect, the permanent, multiracial
opposition, and it has been remarked, somewhat facetiously, that
Julius Nyerere has less trouble keeping it solidly behind him
than the TANU with its exclusively African membership now
up to almost eight hundred thousand.

The former shepherd boy clearly dominates all political life in Tanganyika. His reputation outside his own country was established by his election to head the Pan-African Freedom Movement of East and Central Africa. He sometimes remarks that he cannot get everything he wants in the time he would like. But he points out, "All Africa is impatient; time is important." He is intensely aware of the quick changes taking place in Africa.

An independent Tanganyika, within democratic multiracial lines, is the leader's goal. On December 15, 1959, when London issued its historic announcement that the territory would achieve internal self-government during 1960, the joyous people of Tanganyika chanted *Uhuru*—the Swahili freedom motto of TANU— throughout the day and night. Nyerere's reaction was, "We cannot afford to fail."

The TANU leader has sensed and very frankly discussed the gnawing fear of the European or Indian settler in Africa who has watched the meteoric rise to power of the African himself.

We have fought our battle here against the injustice of a colonial system which qualified the "rights" of an individual according to the color of his skin. Are we now to turn around and deny that principle ourselves by discriminating against those whose skins are *not* black? . . .

Our desire to give confidence to the non-Africans who have made their homes among us is, again, based on a principle: the principle of Human Rights.

I have been asked by visitors to Tanganyika, "How have you people achieved this unity? Why is Tanganyika so different from other mixed territories?" There is one great difference: in Tanganyika the Asians and the Europeans have decided to trust us; in other territories, Nationalist leaders have said exactly what I have said and they have been locked up.

Julius Nyerere has not been locked up for saying such things and there are two main reasons. He has never advocated violence or spoken in terms of hate. He has spoken with restraint and in friendly humor to white audiences. Most important, this man who does not lack for native eloquence, who can whip a group of Kenyans into near-ecstasy, speaks words that have the shocking power of ultimate truth, that reveal a personality that sees the basic problem with a pure, balanced sense of reality.

Discussing the chances for outside economic aid in the first years of Tanganyika's independence, he has warned his people of the rivalries of the givers of aid and the strings attached.

I say these things because we do not want to be misunderstood. It is not from any false pride, or from blindness that we have been telling our people . . . the war against our ignorance, poverty and disease is *our* war. It can only be won by *our own* sweat and toil. It is simply because we have seen the warning of the past; we have seen that it would be unwise to pin our hopes too much on assistance from outside.

This former teacher has the skill not only to anticipate critical problems before they arise, he has the kind of courage that points them out.

In this country, as in most other colonial or ex-colonial "plural societies" of Africa, the economic divisions between rich and poor coincide almost exactly with the divisions between the races. Wherever extreme poverty exists beside a visibly high standard of living there is the risk of bitterness; when the problem is linked with racial differences it is even more potentially dangerous than in a monoracial society. . . . When independence comes, we must tackle this economic complication quickly; if we cannot close the gap rapidly enough, so that the differences in economic status become less glaring and, above all, are freed from their former link with racial divisions, there is a possibility that the potential danger might become a reality, and the economic problem bring us back to the very "race" problem which we claim to have solved.

He sees the key position of his country. Tanganyika's success in solving this dual problem of economic and race relations may well decide, he says, the pattern of the future for the whole of East, Central and Southern Africa.

## The Days Ahead

Julius Nyerere has been the architect of the new African state, Tanganyika. Dedicated, tireless, he has turned his country into an example of what enlightened leadership can do. He has brought his people—Negro, European and Asian—to the doorstep of independence without bloodshed, suffering or even emotional extremes. He has been positive and constructive, abandoning what he himself has called "the politics of complaint." In the days ahead he will meet critical tests of his leadership abilities.

Will the harmonious relationships between the races forged during the preparatory period for independence continue now that the goal has been almost achieved? The leader has added the Swahili word *Kazi*—"toil," to the slogan of *Uhuru*—"freedom," that has been so often on the lips of his people. The belt-tightening that must take place if economic progress is to follow political freedom will require the Tanganyikans to embrace the concept of *Kazi* with the same fervor as their leader.

## We Are All Looking for the Same Mountain

My several friends in Tanganyika took me to the foot of Mt. Kilimanjaro. Overwhelmed by the majesty of the mountain, we sat down on the ground in the cool breezes of the Tanganyikan plain. There were four of us there that afternoon, two Africans and two Americans—two blacks and two whites. As George, the young Tanganyikan labor leader, looked steadfastly up to the top of Mt. Kilimanjaro where the white snow glistened, he said, "In many ways this mountain can be an inspiration for racial harmony. Good men of both races are looking for the same mountain —the mountain of peace and harmony even if from different points of view. Perhaps as we found this mountain this afternoon only through strenuous effort, the whites and blacks in Africa will only find that basis by which they can live through the same determination and effort."

# VI

# Léopold-Sedar Senghor

## The Poet-Philosopher Who Became a Leader of His People

Léopold-Sedar Senghor is the intellectual among African leaders, famed among his colleagues as an eloquent spokesman for their culture and tradition. He is the author of the idea of "negritude" which holds that there is "a mystic union with nature and supernational forces that is an important element of the African way of life." This concept expressed by Mr. Senghor in his essays and poetry of the late 1930's soon became popular among all Negro Africans who were trying to rediscover their roots, regain identity and self-respect. Later, his concept of "negritude" was to provide a philosophical basis for African nationalism.

The man who was to become one of Africa's leading political thinkers was born October 9, 1906, in the farming village of Joal, a hundred miles South of Dakar. His father was a middle-class planter-merchant member of the Sereres, one of the smaller tribes in Senegal. His mother being Christian, Léopold was baptized a Catholic and attended a small missionary school near Joal. The elder Mr. Senghor arranged for the young Léopold to attend the local school as did Léopold's twenty some brothers and sisters. After completing his elementary studies in the village school, he went to Dakar where he received his secondary education at another missionary school. Here again his brilliance was recognized and upon the completion of his secondary education in Senegal he was sent to Paris to attend the university there. While at the University of Paris he majored in language and literary studies. Fame came to him first as an academician. He was the first African to be appointed a professor at the Lycée of Tours in France. Today, Senghor the poet is active in the political arena. On the personal side, he is married and has two teen-age sons and a younger boy. He is a leader of those Africans who believe that the African people should have their own political independence but then should cooperate with their former European administrators. In the case of his own country, Senegal, long occupied by the French, he feels that it is time for his people to direct their own political destinies but he wants them to retain all the good things of French culture. It could be said that he sees no reason why his people should not have the frosting of French connections while they eat the cake of independence. He feels that in the world of interdependence there is an excellent opportunity for the peoples of Europe and Africa, as equals, to cooperate in social, spiritual and cultural matters. Senghor's interest in scholarly matters did not prevent him from turning to active politics. He began first as the political philosopher; then became a political activist.

His eventual commitment to political activity was predestined by his deep interest in his own Senegalese people. Senegal, home of Senghor, has one of the most fascinating histories of all the African countries.

*Senegal*

Senegal, on the west coast of Africa, is approximately the same size as the state of Kansas. The total population of around 2.8 million people is distributed mostly between two tribes: the Wolof people, who are among the darkest peoples in Africa and who were the first to have contact with the French traders. They are now attracted to urban areas and are noticeably active in politics. Along the valley of the Senegal live the Toucouleurs whose society is still headed by feudal chieftainships. Both tribes are Moslem. Slightly more than 90 per cent of the people are Moslem. The remaining less than 10 per cent are Christian—mostly Catholic.

Senegal is a low horseshoe-shaped territory. Were it not for the Senegal River and the line of coastal oases between Dakar and St. Louis, agriculture would be virtually nonexistent. Most of the territory is sparse savanna but the Senegal floods, between July and November, over much of the river valley. In spite of the climatic disadvantages, Senegal derives much of its income from agriculture. The peanut is Senegal's most important export.

From Dakar north, the climate is almost mild rather than tropical. Here the cold Canary's current saves the coast from the more oppressive hot and humid weather typical elsewhere.

There have been inhabitants in Senegal since Neolithic and Paleolithic times. The first known Negro tribe was the Toucouleurs, whose arrival is dated about the ninth century. The modern name for Senegal was derived either from their principal town, Senegara, or from the Zenega Berbers in Mauritania. The Zenegas established themselves about 1040 on the river and converted the Toucouleurs. Later a branch sacked Ghana and conquered Morocco.

By the thirteenth century, however, a pagan invasion eclipsed the Moslem tribes. Senegal was the home of the Wandingos, many of whose descendents became slaves in the United States. By the eighteenth century the Moslem Toucouleurs were able to regain independence and establish a feudal theocracy. Meanwhile, in the fourteenth century, the Wolof, previously subject to the Toucouleurs, had established an independent kingdom. French Norman traders had the earliest contact with West Africa. Their trading posts, however, were abandoned by the fourteen hundreds and by 1444 the Portuguese were active along the West Coast. Here they found a rich source of slaves—and a new field for conversion. As Portuguese influence waned, England entered

Gambia and the French returned to Senegal and commenced effective occupation in 1624. By 1633 the French Senegal Company was formed and a few years later a colony was formed at St. Louis. This soon became the principal center for French influence in Africa.

In 1677 the French captured the island of Gorée from the Dutch and maintained a flourishing trade from the fort there until it was destroyed by the British in 1693. But it was rebuilt under the able direction of André Brue and Gorée flourished again. Brue made notable contributions to French knowledge of the area by exploring the hinterland behind St. Louis and up the Senegal. In the nineteenth century the French decided to establish Senegal as the beachhead for French movement inland. The over-all French plan for Africa called for the French to move east from Senegal and west from French Somalia. Although the plan never materialized it did firmly establish Senegal as the key French area in Africa. By the end of the nineteenth century, the French, by administering through existing local institutions, maintained effective administrative control. In 1904 Senegal was formally recognized as a territory of France.

As a result of this long association, Senegal has received preferential treatment. The Constitution in 1793 abolished slavery and stated, "All men, without distinction of color, domiciled in French colonies, are French citizens and enjoy all rights assured by the Constitution." In 1848 Senegal elected its first deputy to the French Assembly. St. Louis has been a self-governing city since 1872 with a majority of Senegalese as councilors. This elected council had power over the budget and taxes, but the territory was governed by a French-appointed governor aided by a secretary-general and privy council.

### Senghor's Life as an Intellectual

It was from this territory that Léopold-Sedar Senghor was sent hopefully to France. While a student at the University of Paris, he was not long in becoming recognized as one of the most brilliant not only among Africans but all students. Fame came early. Soon after graduation he, an African, was appointed from the University of Paris to be professor at the Lycée of Tours. This was indeed a tribute. Here in addition to his teaching he soon became the spokesman for his continent among the intelligentsia of France and Europe. In poems and essays he gave expression to the longing of the African people for their own cultural identification. He was the first, really, to give written expression to the unique aspects of the African way of life. His writings constantly reaffirmed what to him was its important aspect—the "mystic union with nature and its supernatural forces."

As World War II approached, Senghor, ever loyal to his civic responsibilities, joined the French Infantry, fought in World War II and for a short time was a prisoner of the Germans in France.

One of his great dreams was for a university in Senegal. His concept of a university for West Africa was based on the highest and best traditions of France, adapted to the unique needs of Africa. Finally, in 1952 an institute of higher studies was established. In 1957 this became the University of Dakar which three years later was to boast an enrollment of 1,193 students, 865 of them Africans. In a historic address given by Senghor at the inauguration of the university, he called for Eur-African cooperation so that European and African institutions could work to build a foundation of cooperation and friendship between the European and African peoples.

### Senghor—The Political Leader

Knowing his country and sensing its growing demands for political autonomy, it was natural for Senghor to turn his attention to political matters. Although he had no previous political experience, in 1945 the leaders of the Senegalese Socialist party, needing a strong candidate for a Council position, insisted that he run. This was the start of his political career. From 1945 to 1951 he was busy in the mechanics of local political organization and developing his intellectual talent as applied to leading domestic political and international matters. He soon began to identify himself from the viewpoint of a political philosophy. He describes himself as essentially a socialist who wants to find the "African road to socialism." However, he claims that his socialism is a "socialist method," not a doctrine or even a system. He feels that independence is the only way to rid Africa of the vestiges of colonialism, the social, economic, political and cultural inequalities. But on the other hand, to him independence is not in itself a solution—only the first step.

In a modern world all nations, large and small, are interdependent. Nations must "give up the fictional absolute of independence to enjoy real independence," Senghor declares. He especially believes in a natural cooperation between the neighbors of the Mediterranean, the European powers whom he calls "the northern neighbors," and the southern neighbors, the African powers. Here he talks of Eur-African cooperation but he has always pointed out that this can come only after the African peoples are equal partners, that is, after they have the independent right to direct their own political destiny.

During the early years of his political activity he was especially involved in developing political institutions which would bring forth political autonomy and at the same time assure that all the benefits that Senegal had received from French occupation would remain. Beginning in 1946 Senegal moved quickly in the evolution from a more or less colonial status to semiautonomy. In 1946 the new French Constitution awarded French citizenship to all Africans in French territories. These territories were also represented in the French National Assembly on a limited franchise basis.

In 1951 Senghor faced a key battle for his political life. It was fought over his political philosophy of deliberate peaceful progress toward independence as soon as possible and then continued cooperation and association with France. To the surprise of many political observers he took his message primarily to the rural peoples of Senegal. His opponents felt that he, an intellectual and a Christian, would have little chance with the poorer farmers, mostly illiterate and Moslem. He received an overwhelming majority in the election which established him as the strongest political leader in Senegal. Two years later, in 1953, as a recognized powerful African political leader, he proposed the revision of the Constitution to make France and the overseas territories a federation of equal parts—the overseas territories partners in federation with France.

On March 31, 1957, French Africans voted in their first general election. Under the provision of the *loi-cadre*, which gave French African states greater autonomy, they voted primarily for representatives to the territorial assemblies. Senghor had some reservations regarding the *loi-cadre* because he felt it loosed the federal ties that existed among the territories of French West Africa. He feared it was another divide-and-rule tactic. The Convention Africaine (CA) originated in the Senegalese popular bloc headed by Senghor and was aimed at regrouping all the political parties in French Black Africa into a single political organization. It was particularly strong in Senegal. Under Senghor the CA received 8 per cent of the total number of votes in French West Africa and won seventy-seven seats altogether in French West Africa and French Equatorial Africa which made it a minority opposition party. Senghor who, as a scholar, always advocated cultural cooperation, was now as a leader working for political cooperation among the groups in French West Africa.

Senghor was a leader at the conference of African parties in Dakar in March, 1958, which marked the birth of the Parti du Régroupement Africain (PRA). His party was essentially socialist in orientation. As a party leader, Senghor sat on the Consultative Committee for de Gaulle's Constitution. During negotiations he pressed for provisions granting African independence first and then machinery for confederation with France, but could extract only a compromise allowing federation within the new community. Although this did not meet his original demands he finally accepted de Gaulle's Constitution. In the referendum of 1958 he played a leading role in advocating that the people of Senegal vote in favor of the French Community. As a leader of the PRA he was instrumental in obtaining an amazing 97 per cent support of the community for de Gaulle.

## The de Gaulle Plan

Under the 1958 Constitution there was only one citizenship in the community and all citizens of the community were equal before the law. By voting "yes" territories became member states (autonomous republics) and were self-governing in all matters except foreign policy, common defense, currency, common economic and financial policy. These powers were to be reserved to the community. The community would also retain control of higher education, courts and interstate and foreign communication. By community was meant not the French government but the governmental institutions—an executive council, a senate and a court of arbitration, common to all the member states including France. Territories also had the option of immediate full independence, to become a department of France or to assume the position of an overseas territory of France. A further measure stipulated that a member state could change status within the community or sever its ties completely at any time. The nature of the community as defined in its first article was rather vague. It was a political organization based on the equality and solidarity of the people who, by an act of free determination, adopted the Constitution of 1958.

The overwhelming support given by the people of Senegal to the adoption of the 1958 Constitution greatly strengthened Senghor's position not only in Senegal but throughout French Africa.

Once the 1958 Constitution had been adopted, Senghor immediately began to work for his goal of eventual independence for the people of Senegal. While attempting to realize these goals he also had to face increasing opposition from the "Young Turks" of Senegal who wanted immediate independence even if by violent means and were not especially interested in subsequent cooperation with France. Once the 1958 Constitution was adopted, Senghor's three goals were:

1. Immediate independence.
2. A federation of the former French territories of Africa.
3. A multinational confederation with France.

Realizing that real independence would be impossible without French guarantees of economic support, Senghor began to encourage the development of the Mali Federation. At the Bamako Conference in December, 1958—only a few months after the adoption of the French Constitution—he played a lead role in developing the concept of the Mali Federation which united for a brief time the autonomous republics of Senegal and Sudan.

The year 1959 was a busy one for Senghor. Since he had fought to create the Mali Federation he now had to provide leadership in developing the institutions of cooperation for these two autonomous republics. In the fall of 1959 he developed the basis of the transfer of sovereign powers from France to the Mali Federation. Essentially the negotiations provided that while the Mali Federation would take over the sovereign attribute of its own defense, France would maintain military bases there, Mali would remain in the French monetary and customs union and French would be the official language of the new nation. Final negotiations for the transfer of sovereignty from France to the Mali Federation took place in Paris in January and February, 1960. The Mali Federation, while remaining closely linked to France, became fully sovereign in June, 1960.

His new dream, the Mali Federation, was immediately hit with difficulties. The principal problem was the difference between the Senegalese, steeped in over a century of democratic traditions, and the Soudanese, long accustomed to a strong, mono-lithic type of government.

When it became apparent that a working basis between the two partners in the Federation could not be maintained, Senegal withdrew from the Federation and declared her independence on August 20, 1960, as the Republic of Senegal. A few weeks later Léopold-Sedar Senghor was elected as the first President of the new republic.

## Senghor and the Future

Léopold-Sedar Senghor, President of the Republic of Senegal, is in the middle of the great political changes taking place in Africa. To Senghor the interests of the French-speaking African states, now independent, can best be served by maintaining cultural and economic ties with France. Essentially still a poetic idealist, President Senghor has faith that at this point in history, if European-African cooperation can be worked out as expressed in his idea of it, a new dawn for the African and European peoples will arise.

# VII

## Sékou Touré—
## The Man Who Chose
## Independence

As the broad-shouldered, articulate and personable young President of the Republic of Guinea, Sékou Touré, walked with me to the door of his office upon the completion of our conversation, my mind went back to his address at the United Nations on November 5, 1959, when he said:

Populations which include more than 80 per cent of illiterate peasants, with an annual individual income of less than one hundred dollars, and therefore, with the most precarious conditions of life—these are the harsh realities of Africa, when it is no longer masked behind the ridiculous veil of exoticism which hides from unaware eyes the colossal misery of our vast underdeveloped countries at present sparsely populated because of centuries of slavery.

And yet in this poverty, of which humanity should be ashamed, there is man, with his invisible faith in the destiny of humanity; there is his hope, his determination to win and to grow; his immense spiritual brotherhood and harmony, his kindness still in its purest form; and at the same time his extraordinary energy and sharp sense of responsibility. There is also the incalculable amount of virtues and values of almost two hundred million Africans, the tremendous possibilities which this represents and the intellectual potential which this may hold.

When he grasped my hand and said, "*A bientôt*" I felt that here was the man who would try in every way, as he had told the United Nations, to end this poverty "of which humanity should be ashamed" for his people.

Sékou Touré was born in 1922 at Faranah, a town on the banks of the Niger now known as Djoliba. His parents, Alpha and Aminata Touré, were respected, hard-working, but relatively poor farmers. One of seven children, he attended a school of Koranic studies at Kankan and later went to a French technical school. While attending the technical school he also carried on his secondary studies by correspondence courses. There is something of the Horatio Alger hero in his story. He received his first job in 1940 at the age of eighteen when he was employed as a clerk by a local business firm. Within a year, however, he passed the examination which qualified him for employment as an administrative clerk in the Post and Telecommunications Department of the French government. While his friends engaged in the usual activities of teen-age boys, Sékou Touré read voraciously. Unable to receive proper recognition in his Post Office position from the French government, he moved to the Treasury Department. While there, he reached the conclusion that there was little room for him in the French Colonial Service for Guineans, and resigned his position to become a full-time labor organizer and leader. In those early years of union work, Sékou Touré demonstrated the organizing ability of the man who wishes to resolve the immediate problems of the workers rather than the approach of the long-range planner or theorist. He soon became the full-time head of the Guinea branch of France's General Confederation of Labor. It was the work of this union which took him to France and later to Warsaw and Prague. While in Europe he indicated that he was impressed with the systems of both the European socialist and the Marxist nations. He felt that something from each system might be adapted to the needs of Africa.

*The Country*

Some believe that President Touré's determination to attack the problems of the most wretched of his people springs from the background of the country in which he was reared.

The tribal inhabitants of Guinea are the Fulas, Susus and Jalonkes. These three tribes equal five-sixths of the population of Guinea. They have absorbed many characteristics of the Mandingos, a tribe of once great stature. There are about 2.7 million people inhabiting Guinea's 105,000 square miles—an area about the size of the state of Oregon.

The Guinea coast is one of the wettest spots of Africa. Rainfall varies from 80 to a fantastic 150 inches a year. The coast is jagged and rocky. It is about 30 miles wide and 200 miles long. Palms and bananas grow along the coastal belt in the midst of coarse grass, mangrove, woodland and scrub pine. Moving inland, the country changes to rolling foothills covered with grass and woodland. These are the foothills of the Futa Jallon, a mountainous chain running northwest-southwest that divides Guinea from Sierra Leone. These mountains range from 3,000 to 6,000 feet in the southwest. Both the Niger and the Senegal have their sources here. The Futa Jallon is one of the most prosperous agricultural belts in West Africa. The mountains slope northeast to grass and woodlands but give way to drier savanna and desert farther east. Peanuts, sesame seed, fruit, cotton, sisal, kola, coffee, cocoa, cattle and sheep are all raised in Guinea. Millets, rice and maize, however, are the chief staples. The principal exports are bananas, palm products, kola nuts, gum rubber and sesame seed.

The modern history of Guinea is supposed to date from A.D. 700 with the legendary killing of the Songhai River god by the founder of the Za dynasty. "Za" had its origins in the east, perhaps Egypt or Arabia. Songhai (the kingdom) flourished under the Zas and even though conquered by Mali in 1325, its influence spread to Timbuktu in the Niger headwaters. The Za dynasty was succeeded by the Sonni dynasty proclaimed by two Songhai brothers of noble blood. They had been taken captive and reared in the Mali court. But in 1355 they escaped dramatically to restore Songhai glory. The last of this line, Sonni Ali, was the first great Songhai king. He completely revitalized the government and the culture. His reign, ending in 1493, brought great intellectual advance and material prosperity to Songhai. The fame of the scholars at Timbuktu and Jenné attracted students throughout the ancient world and a whole literature developed there in the sixteenth and seventeenth centuries. During his reign, Sonni Ali dominated the western Sudan. He was a man of great administrative ability but of extreme temperament. Only the humane intercession of the king's adviser, Mohammed Abou Bekr, saved many from the king's wrath.

It was this minister who succeeded Sonni Ali. He was a Moslem with great respect for religion and learning. Under Mohammed's able administration there was a Moslem revival (Sonni Ali hated the Moslems and only his contradictory nature can explain his attachment to Mohammed) and great intellectual development. Trade expanded and the kingdom dominated an area almost to the ocean and into Hausaland. Mohammed assumed the name of Askia and his dynasty ruled until the Songhai was overrun by the Moors. Fruitless and wasteful civil wars among Mohammed's descendants contributed to the weakening and final collapse of Songhai in 1545.

While the Phoenician traders did have limited contact with this part of West Africa, the first real European penetration was made by the Portuguese under the direction of Prince Henry. These Portuguese explorers were interested in the rumored wealth of the African forests. Portugal, however, was never interested in West Africa except for trading purposes and as her power in Europe declined, she was expelled from her West African trading posts by the French and the British and the Dutch in the middle seventeenth century. These powers maintained posts for trade only—particularly the slave trade. It was not until 1770 that any exploration of the interior was attempted. Mungo Park traveled up the Gambia to the Niger and died in an attempt to follow the river to its mouth. The Barth expedition of 1850 opened up the Sudan and Chad areas.

The empire splintered into many remnants of native kingdoms which also indulged in internecine warfare. Such was the condition when the French arrived and pacified the disunified states.

Guinea was one of the first areas to fall under colonial domination in the "mad scramble" of European powers, drawn by the wealth in gold, ivory, pepper, oils, precious woods and stones. The Guinea part of the African melon was assigned (through informal agreement first, later formalized at the Berlin Conference of 1884–1885) to the French. The only real obstacle to the French occupation of this area was Samori Touré, whose campaigns were waged against them throughout the present Ivory Coast and Guinea territory. He finally retreated to the Futa Jallon where he was captured in 1906. Little did the French know that within a few decades another Touré, Samori's descendant, would arise and bring independence to his people.

The administrative goal of the French occupation of Guinea was similar to that in other areas of Africa occupied by France—permanent association legally and administratively between France and her overseas territories. Until 1946 the administration consisted primarily of direct French rule through local leaders or chiefs.

### Sékou Touré—His Early Leadership Period

It was against this background of pre-1946 French administration of Guinea that Sékou Touré was reared. During his early years his friends recognized him as a brilliant organizer, an effective speaker and a tireless worker. These talents and energies were devoted during these early years to the immediate needs of his fellow workers. Furthermore, if he had wished to engage

in political activity in those days it would have been quite difficult under the French administration. His political career was
launched when he organized and won a general strike lasting
seventy-six days. This strike brought the first major concessions
to the workers of French West Africa. By birth and background,
Sékou Touré is both a fighter and a leader. In appearance today,
he might be a successful college fullback, ten years after graduation. His rise up the political ladder was quick. In 1951 he won
a seat in the French National Assembly but was prevented from
taking it. Winning it again in 1954, he charged that the French
had falsified the election. When he was again prevented from
taking his seat, riots ensued. The next year he was overwhelm-
ingly elected Mayor of Conakry and in 1956 he was finally officially elected to the National Assembly. He became the first
territorial Councilor for Conakry and later in that year, a Grand
Councilor for French West Africa. By the end of 1957 he was
Vice President of the Governmental Council of Guinea which in
fact meant operating Head of State.

Under the *loi-cadre* the French kept control of their overseas
territories through French governors but gave the Africans the
right to elect the operating heads and gave them far greater
autonomy. Although his powers as Vice President were limited,
Monsieur Touré made excellent use of them in limiting the
powers of the chiefs and setting up more than four thousand village councils elected by universal suffrage. In this move he eliminated the "chieftaincy" institution which had held back progress
among the Africans for hundreds of years and he set up the beginning of a dynamic political organization.

Within a few months after the establishment of the *loi-cadre*
in 1956, Monsieur Touré and his associates made no secret of the
fact that this new system was only the first step in an irreversible
process. He immediately proceeded to bring about the next step
by going to Paris where he informed the French government officials that the Guineans came to "make the law." Actually, to the

well informed observers of the Guinean scene the oveiwhelming choice of the Guinean people to seek independence in the French referendum of 1958 was really no surprise since Touré before had made no secret of his and his people's determination to seek complete independence. As a matter of fact, shortly before the French announced their plan for the referendum, he attacked the whole idea of a French union because it would continue the Guinean in a status of "perpetual dependence . . . indignity . . . subordination."

When General de Gaulle visited Conakry on his tour of Africa before the referendum, he heard Monsieur Touré declare in his presence, "We prefer poverty in liberty to riches in slavery." Several weeks later the people of Guinea gave Sékou Touré a thunderous endorsement by voting a 95 per cent "No" to the French Constitution. Sékou Touré had led his people to independence.

Immediately following the referendum on September 28, 1958, the Guinean leader tried a rapprochement with General de Gaulle: "Guinea is loyally holding out her hand to the nation that dominated her." He wanted some kind of ties with France on the basis of an association of independent states but de Gaulle evidently could not politically afford to allow Guinean defection without punishment. He pulled out four thousand French officials and stopped the nearly eighty-million-dollar investment program. In his note, de Gaulle said, "Guinea can no longer nominally receive any aid from the French state either for administration or for funds for equipment."

## Sékou Touré and Independence

On October 2, 1958, Sékou Touré proclaimed the independence of the Republic of Guinea. The man who chose independence for a country which until that time was relatively unknown was to say a few months later:

African history in our days is undergoing such an acceleration that decisive and important events punctuate the process at an unexpected rhythm. Only ten years ago Africa was almost entirely occupied by foreigners and its life regulated for their exclusive profit. Africa was absent from the international scene. Today the representatives of some ten African nations, as members of various international organizations, express the fraternal will of their sovereign people. Soon other nations will accede to liberty.

The most significant fact is the massive and general uprising of all our peoples, even those who until now have been considered the most backward, that is, the most oppressed. All the plans to restrain this fierce will of Africa for the reconquest of its dignity are being frustrated one way or another, and always it is the same burning cry that echoes across our entire continent: independence. Thus, independence and unity today are the two irresistible forces which are shaking Africa.

Now that he is a figure on the international stage, various questions are raised about Monsieur Touré. What are his political aspirations? What kind of political organization does he follow? What are his ideological leanings? How does he feel about the question of a United States of Africa?

President Touré has given to us some of the answers to these questions. Since he had no lycée or university training in Africa or France, he has been little influenced by French traditions and culture. As a young man he was oriented to the pragmatic problems of the workers. His earliest drives were to do something for his fellow Guineans. He recognized the trade union movement as a means of doing this. In his youth he was essentially interested in quick and dramatic change. He knew the change could only be for the better for the Guineans on the lowest rung of the ladder.

In his trade union activities he soon became recognized as a nationalist. But his nationalism came after his interest in trade unionism. His interest in trade unionism resulted from his desire to change by dramatic improvement the daily lot of his peoples. As a trade union official, he was known as a meticulous organizer. He has carried this ability over into politics. The secret of his success has come from organizing right down to the village level. His party defined it as "unity of concept and unity of action from top to bottom in the condition and form decided by the militant masses." Touré later said, "When it comes to agitation, our past experiences leave us in fear of no one. We have been violent and we shall be violent again if necessary."

The Parti Démocratique de Guinée is the party organized by Touré. He claims that his system of one party is complete democracy because it is organized from the base to the summit. Within the party there is one committee for every six hundred men and women, or a total of four thousand local committees. The committees are elected each year. When the author discussed this procedure with the President's younger brother, Ismael Touré, it was pointed out by him that "complete democracy" existed within this one party and therefore there was no need for additional parties. Under this system, parliament is an institution for the legalization of party decisions. All discussion takes place within the framework of the party; there is practically no discussion in the parliament.

This political development actually follows quite closely Sékou Touré's earlier comments on politics. During his visit to Europe in 1946 he indicated that his own political value system was close to socialism. He felt that one party was best suited to his needs because Guinea, like much of Africa, was not ready for the multi-party systems of Western Europe. One party, in his opinion, would assure these three political needs for the new African states: strong leadership, carefully defined objectives and precise instructions on how to fulfill these objectives. It is well to remember that this thinking grew out of a pre-de Gaulle background in which the weak and fluttering governments of postwar Paris were a poor example of the multiparty system. When President Touré was recently asked about the possibility of developing a two-party system in Guinea, he replied:

It would be necessary for the conditions of an opposition to exist. For the moment they do not. Guinea's political unity has been proved by the referendum and has been growing stronger ever since. It is not our intention to squander this chance of unity by adopting a system which would only reduce our political strength. What Africa needs is a fundamental revolution. It is not too much to ask that all our strength be mobilized and directed toward a common goal. A political system based on two parties would be a certain check on our evolution. The revolutionary dynamism doesn't need any other stimulant than our needs, our aspirations and our hopes.

President Touré's views about the desirability of the one-party system have caused some observers to call him a Communist. This would seem inaccurate when a close observation indicates that his preference for a one-party system stems from his basic political value system: a practical approach to the problem of his people. "Man is not made for philosophy. The people don't have to adore any philosophy whatever. Efficacy is measured in the sum of the possibilities offered to the people for the solution of problems. In Africa there is neither a socialist nor a radical nor a popular republican. There are simply men and groups of men with different labels who envisage the same objectives in the distant future and who use different methods at present according to their education in economic, political and social context that conditions them," he says.

"It is evident that certain Marxist concepts suit African conditions, but it is no less evident that Africa will have to find its own revolutionary principles. As for the class problems, you will note that there exists in Africa one and the same class—that of the dispossessed." While he does not feel that the capitalist system would solve the problems of the people of Guinea, he has publicly stated that a chief need of Guinea is lots of foreign capital.

To date he has been unsuccessful in attracting support from any direction except Russia and the Soviet satellites which apparently see in Guinea an economical spot from which to spread the news of the Communist "heaven on earth."

Essentially Sékou Touré has worked for the establishment of a political personality for his country and to begin the great push upward in combating illiteracy, poverty and disease. In commenting on this situation, the New York *Times* declared:

Sékou Touré is insisting that Guinea is lined up with neither East nor West, wants no part of that conflict and must be judged on the basis of its own actions, not someone else's ideology. If Guinea during its first year has been deluged with trade missions, with cultural missions and with every other kind of mission from the Soviet world—the door is equally open to similar advances from the non-Soviet world. As in the case of other emerging African states, Guinea will take material and moral assistance wherever it is offered. . . . The political organization of the new African nations must necessarily spring out of the African context. They cannot be expected to start off as full blown Western style parliamentary democracies. We can do much to help them develop in that direction, however, primarily by helping them to improve their standard of living, and not by insisting that they follow a preconceived ideological patent.

After several years in office, President Touré still declares he is just as opposed to all forms of colonialism as he was in his early days fighting for independence. In his 1959 address to the United Nations he denounced colonialism in scathing terms. He declared, "Colonialism may put up buildings and factories, bridges and ports, but it can only crush and divide the peoples by degrading man."

Seeking to "alert" the United Nations against colonial operations still under way in Africa, President Touré said that "colonialists" through "their Machiavellian plan" still aim at dividing Africa so that they may remain the "masters of the continent." He emphasized that unity is necessary for the safety and survival of the independent African countries. In this same UN address he publicly appeals to France, England, Belgium, Portugal and Spain to "raise their conscience to a level of the interdependent interests of humanity" and help Africa "to liberate itself from the colonial force, from social misery and indignity." He went on and called for a real application for the principle of self-determination, "without trickery or maneuvers, without illusionary façades."

Even though Guinea has only recently achieved its independence, its government officials are already thinking about the rest of Africa. A ranking minister said, "We cannot be truly independent unless all Africa is independent," and added, "We want to stay out of the East-West quarrel."

## The Future

The one word that will probably describe the immediate future of the Republic of Guinea will be change. The political personality of the Republic must, in the words of President Touré, be developed as soon as possible. Furthermore, gigantic strides must be made in conquering the great enemies of the Guinean people—poverty, illiteracy and disease.

In developing the personality of Guinea, Touré and his advisers have deliberately taken steps to cut off the social, cultural and economic ties that have existed between their country and France. In this, he is unique. Guinea has pulled out of the franc zone and established its own currency. More and more of its exports, traditionally directed to France and Western Europe are being sold to the Communist countries behind the Iron Curtain. The Communist countries for their part, are actively engaged in technical assistance programs in Guinea. Since 1958, eight permanent Communist-bloc diplomatic and trade missions have been established in Guinea. Trade agreements have been concluded with Bulgaria, Poland, East Germany, Hungary and Czechoslovakia. These agreements cover nearly 25 per cent of Guinea's total external trade.

The few years since 1958 have also seen drastic changes in

some aspects of Guinea's educational programs. Formerly the young men of Guinea who went abroad for studies attended one of the universities or training programs in France. Since independence, few have gone to France; over two hundred are in the Communist countries and almost two hundred are studying at the University of Dakar in Senegal.

Unlike some of the pioneer leaders of other continents, Africans seem to have a sense of humor. President Touré, when he was treated to a ticker tape parade up Broadway during his United States visit, was asked to comment on the fact that New York City had mistakenly put flags of Ghana on the lamp posts. The President of Guinea seemed honestly to think it was funny.

In his talk at the National Press Club in Washington, he urged that when American and Russian scientists were "concentrating on the moon, . . . Africa would ask that you think of development on this planet—Africa is still on this planet."

Sékou Touré has emerged as the African leader who advocates not only political independence but also cultural, social and economic separation from the former colonial powers. He feels, he says, that only in this way can the African peoples develop their own true individuality.

Touré declares that African nations must not align themselves with either bloc in the present East-West power struggle. On the other hand, since the needs of Africa are so great, he feels that they should take the best from all economic and social systems— both the Western system and Marxism. In addition to systems, he says that his people should be able to accept the much-needed assistance from any state without being identified with the policies of that state.

In my recent visit to Guinea, I was told that there was only one reason for the economic aid from the Communist countries so visible in Conakry (a high-speed, modern printing plant is one of the significant contributions)—it was given to the people of Guinea and they will take aid without strings from any one.

Some raise the question of Monsieur Touré's ability to maintain the course of complete political, cultural and economic independence without aligning his country with any of the power blocs. While it is too early to predict the future direction of the Republic of Guinea, it seems to this writer that Sékou Touré, the man who chose independence for his people after years of struggle, is not going to barter willingly this independence for what is well described as the new colonialism, the colonialism of high-powered infiltration and subversion. On the other hand, in September, 1960, when President Touré visited Communist China, he indicated a high regard for their "political-economic system." He also received extensive promises of aid from the Peiping government.

### Africans Believe in God

On a sunny afternoon in Conakry, I visited the local bookstore known as having mostly Communist literature. I found the usual books present in such libraries. There were also quite a few young Guineans browsing around the bookshelves. When I left a young man came with me. Since we were near a coffee shop, I invited him to coffee. We chatted about a variety of subjects—nothing of real importance. After an hour or so I had to leave to keep another appointment. When I got up to go and I shook his hand and said, "Au revoir," he said to me, "Don't worry too much about the Communist bookstore. The Communists have made one big mistake. A great number of their books abuse God and say nasty things about Him. We Africans just naturally believe in a Supreme Being—we believe in some kind of God, perhaps the Christian God, the Moslem Allah or it may be the God in the mountains, but we believe in God and there are very few of us who could ever embrace, philosophically speaking, Marxist communism."

# VIII

# William V. S. Tubman—
# A New Deal for Liberia

When William V. S. Tubman took the oath of office as President of Liberia on January 3, 1944, there was little to indicate that his administration would be responsible for vast social, economic and political improvements for the Liberian people. When he was sworn in again as President in 1960, William Vacanarat Shadrach Tubman had clearly established himself as the man who had done more for Liberia than any man in its history. Now sixty-four, he was born at Harper in Maryland County of his native Liberia. His father, Alexander Tubman, was a former senator, former Speaker of the House of Representatives, and a distinguished Methodist preacher. Both sides of the President's family immigrated from Georgia but his father's family originally were slaves of a Baltimore man who had moved to Augusta. President Tubman's mother was one of the few American Negroes to come to Liberia after the Civil War, arriving in Liberia in 1872.

During the first six years in office he accomplished, in terms of Liberia's history, two remarkable achievements:

1. Full citizenship rights were extended in practice as well as in theory to the native Liberians, especially those in the hinterlands who had been excluded previously from the body politic.

2. He embarked upon a highly imaginative program to pro-

mote his country's economic progress by "the open-door policy" of attracting foreign investment capital.

During his administration the national budget has climbed from $750,000 to its present annual level of slightly more than $20,000,000. Some might say that this development was bound to come and that Tubman has been fortunate enough to hop onto a climbing star but, in fact, economists who knew the area were predicting in 1944 a sharp postwar slump. Tubman averted this by bringing Liberia into the dollar zone and encouraging foreign investment. Luck was a factor but as they say, "a smart man gets lucky" and even the most skeptical would admit that Liberia's development would have come neither as fast nor as far without him. When President Tubman leaves office Liberia will be immensely richer than when he came. His third and last great contribution has been the evolution of his doctrine of Pan-Africanism known as "the Associated States of Africa." He is an advocate of "that type of solidarity which is based on treaties and conventions of friendship, amity, navigation, trade and other alliances on the basis of mutual respect and equal consideration for all." Taking into consideration the differing economic systems, political allegiances and preferences, cultural backgrounds and social customs, President Tubman regards the various bids for Pan-African unity as "unrealistic and utopian." He is fearful that "any hasty or superficial semblance of unity in areas where conflicting issues are not carefully resolved may undermine the entire structure of any permanent political unity and retard real cooperative effort." President Tubman sees his Associated States of Africa as a loose federation providing for consultation on matters of common interest and as machinery for the peaceful solution of disputes between members. Within this federation he advocates the recognition and creation of regional health authorities, research institutes and cultural centers. He also favors a uniform reduction of tariffs and the creation of something approaching a common market.

As I sat in President Tubman's office discussing with him his various plans for the Liberian people, I felt that this man, who has done so much, has never received the credit due to one who has led his people from a completely backward, socially inferior position, to the present much higher sociopolitical and economic level.

### Liberia—The Country

Liberia, until recently the only independent country of West Africa, was founded in 1822 as a home for repatriated slaves. The establishment of this country resulted from the successful efforts of the American Colonization Society to repatriate "free people of color" then living in the United States or freed at sea from captured slavers. The present population of Liberia is officially estimated to be 2.75 million although some sources estimate less than that. Its 43,000 square miles is about equal to the size of the state of Ohio.

As a tribute to United States President James Monroe, a one-time president of the Society, the pioneers named their first settlement Monrovia. During the first few years the settlers were troubled with disease, antagonistic tribesmen and low morale. A courageous New England minister, Jehudi Ashmun, regarded as the founder of Liberia, led the struggling community successfully against the tribesmen. Ashmun, a white, was for a time joined by the Reverend Robert Gurley, who is credited with suggesting the name "Liberia" for the new colony. As Monrovia consolidated itself, other settlements were made and in 1833, the "Independent African State of Maryland" was founded at Cape Palmas. In 1857 it was annexed to Liberia as Maryland County. Most of the settlers, however, arrived before 1825 during the "great migrations." By that time there were twenty thousand original settlers. There were no further migrations.

From 1822 on, the colonies were confronted with constant wars and revolts among the tribes. These revolts spread to the interior and Liberia, lacking sufficient force, could barely control the outbreaks. In 1858, 1875, 1910 and 1915, American aid was sought to quell the Kru risings. This coastal tribe had long harassed the settlers who were also confronted with disease and one of the most difficult climates in Africa. The rainfall over the coast and for about a hundred and twenty miles inland is equatorial, in the western half of the country being about one hundred and fifty inches and in the eastern half about one hundred inches. Adverse climatic conditions coupled with constant warfare and an unwillingness to work, plunged the colony into despair.

The last of the white governors died in 1841. His successor, Joseph Jenkins Roberts, a citizen from Virginia, became Liberia's first president. An able administrator, Roberts built Liberia and gave her her first international status. Since the colony was first founded by an independent American society, the country was in an ambiguous national status. The United States government had no jurisdiction over it and acted only as a protector. Although the Society financially assisted the colony, it was in no position to defend it. In particular, France and Britain, whose interests were already established on the Guinea coast, denied the right of the colonists to exercise sovereign power. Consequently, in 1847, Liberia was proclaimed a republic.

Difficulties confronting the new republic were enormous. Because they were unable to control the coast or subdue the inland tribes, illicit slave trade continued. And when British cruisers assumed the task of suppressing the slavers, their presence in Liberian waters threatened the defenseless sovereignty of the country. Furthermore, the republic had constant border troubles with France and England who were extending their influences inland from Sierra Leone and the Ivory Coast. Liberia was practically without revenue and though it tried to control the interior, it was rarely effective beyond twenty miles inland. Not until 1885 and 1892 were treaties with England and France signed fixing the borders.

During this "century for survival" Liberia's major source of support came from American Christian missionaries, particularly in health and education. And the United States played a crucial role as financial backer and recognized protector.

President Roberts remained in office from 1847 until 1856. During this time party lines were forming and Roberts was ousted when his Whig party lost the vote. The Whig party distrusted European encroachment and wanted to develop along national lines. This meant no assistance from the European powers. Roberts' opponents sought cooperation with Europe and desired loans to speed development. His successor, E. J. Royce, did eventually negotiate a loan in London. His opponents feared he would use it to establish himself as a dictator. Royce was deposed and imprisoned and drowned while attempting to escape to a British warship. Roberts was called back to office in 1871 and died in 1876.

Unfortunately, Roberts' death marked the end of an era for Liberia. He had replaced indifference and despair with industry and the nucleus for agricultural development—rubber and coffee farming. The second generation lacked the industry and skills of their fathers. The settler population stagnated into an unproductive aristocracy. Work was done by imported labor and only politics was an acceptable supplement to leisure. The twenty thousand Americo-Liberians monopolized the government to the exclusion of nearly two million other inhabitants. Not until President Arthur Barclay was some effort made to cooperate with the tribes.

Nor were President Barclay's international problems less severe. The French, demanding security from raids across the border, eventually extracted two thousand square miles from Liberia, territory France was unable to control. Germany, too, sent a gunboat to Monrovia over financial matters. The United States, being placed in an awkward spot, demanded reforms. In 1909 an American commission recommended financial changes, negotiated a loan and sent troops to patrol the borders. An American was placed as financial adviser to the government and, as security against the loan, custom duties and some taxes were administered by an American Receiver General. Thus finances were in American hands.

World War I, however, prevented any significant changes and the United States Senate failed to approve a postwar loan. At the same time, the Firestone Rubber Company was investigating the possibilities of plantation farming and the company was granted a concession of one million acres in 1926. The agreement also included a loan to the Liberian government. Firestone's entry into the Liberian economy was to prove an important factor in the country's stability and development.

Paradoxically, however, Liberia almost foundered on the very rock that formed the country—slavery. In 1929, as a member of the League of Nations (she had declared war on Germany in 1917), Liberia was charged with forced labor and slavery. A League study commission reported that Vice President Yancey was guilty of organizing and benefiting from forced labor contracts to the Gabon and Fernando Po. President Charles D. B. King, who had been elected president in 1920, resigned in 1931 along with Vice President Yancey. But the League, under the leadership of Britain and with the consent of the United States, refused to recognize the new regime unless the government made immediate reforms. There was even some discussion of Liberia being administered by an international supervisory board. But diplomatic finesse again saved independence for West Africa's only republic. President King's successor was Edwin James Barclay who became president in December, 1930. He complied with the League's wishes to outlaw slavery, but was still confronted by financial problems and chronic underdevelopment. It was not until 1939 that Liberia saw any real improvement in her economic situation. Her strategic position during the war brought her direct benefits. The United States built what is now Roberts

Airfield, roads and port facilities, and as a participant in the war (Liberia declared war on Germany in January, 1944) she was eligible for lend-lease. By 1944 with President Tubman's election, Liberia was on the way to what approached political stability.

## Early Life of President Tubman

William Tubman's early days were spent in his country's darkest period. Misunderstood by most of her neighbors, Liberia was also shunned by most of the members of the world community of nations. The future president received his education at Cape Palmas Seminary and Cuttington Collegiate and Divinity School. He finished his formal education in 1913 but studied law on his own for the next seven years while holding down a high-school teaching job. Shad, as his friends called him, served as a court recorder, collector of internal revenue and county attorney of Harper until, at the age of twenty-eight, he became the youngest senator in Liberia's history. As an officer in the Liberian frontier force, he had participated in suppressing the bloody Sasstown uprising in 1910, the Bolobo campaign of 1915 and the Glaro expedition of 1917.

Although his abilities were recognized, many of the old guard feared that he had radical (in the Liberian context) tendencies and, in 1937, he was shunted to the Supreme Court as an associate justice. He had made his first trip abroad in 1928 when he visited Kansas City as delegate to a church conference.

During my visit to Monrovia I had an opportunity to see the rambling, four-story Executive Mansion, occupying the central block in the city where President Tubman lives with his wife Antoinette, a granddaughter of former President Arthur Barclay (1904–1912). Mr. Tubman has five children and one of his sons attended Harvard University.

*President Tubman as a Political Leader*

Eventually his merit could no longer be denied and as a member of the True Whig party, he was elected to the presidency on May 4, 1943, and inaugurated January 3, 1944. One of his first acts as President was to declare war on Germany. In April, 1944, he signed the Charter of the United Nations and has since been a strong supporter of that international organization. It is apparent that President Tubman felt his chief problem after he entered office to be narrowing the gap between the Americo-Liberians and the native tribesmen. His initial integration plea called for a "national unification program"—equal opportunity in schools, jobs, wages and social contacts for all Liberians. Tubman claimed that this integration would lessen "social tensions at home and increase Liberia's prestige abroad." To carry out his program, he began by urging legislation for adult suffrage to the aborigines in 1945. This gave them representation in the House of Representatives. He made periodic trips into the interior personally counseling with local chiefs and judging their disputes. He woos the tribes by appearing in their tribal dress. In giving representation to the interior tribes, he declared, "All the people in the interior pay a hut tax. As a matter of principle, we will not tolerate taxation without representation." Today the Americo-Liberians no longer have a monopoly in government positions and are increasingly willing to accept tribesmen into their social circles. By 1947 President Tubman had extended the franchise to women and a year later instituted land reforms. He was now becoming known as the president who was bringing quick and gigantic changes to the Liberian social scene.

President Tubman pushed his unification program with great force. He declared that all those who opposed the program were, in fact, "enemies of the state." After unification he proposes "integration" of all tribes into Liberian society. It is now out of vogue to be racist or even an Americo-Liberian. President Tubman immediately concerned himself with the development of his country. While his predecessors may also have been concerned, they all felt that economic development was out of their reach. Education was seen as a means of getting away from dependence on agriculture, but there were no opportunities created for private investment in industry. Because most young people became lawyers, few were trained as administrators, technicians or business executives. As the Liberians say, they did not receive the benefits of colonialism either in the training of personnel or the building of public works for which they did not have to pay directly. To date Liberia has achieved development without grants-in-aid and she has paid for everything she has received. Now the "open door" policy of President Tubman is encouraging foreign as well as local investment. In 1944 Liberia's revenues were less than one million dollars yearly. By 1959 they were slightly more than twenty million dollars. Before the war only Firestone pioneered Liberia's resources and opportunities. Now there are at least two dozen American companies in Liberia plus several European countries extracting natural resources, seeking agricultural concessions and building communications. The Liberian Mining Company has shipped 2,250,000 tons of ore from the Bomi mines and is now developing the Nimbu deposits. In 1954 the Import-Export Bank lent Liberia $6,250,000 and the United States gave $4,000,000 for technical assistance. President Tubman feels that his open-door policy is the key to major development of Liberia's mineral resources. This has been made easier by Liberia's removal of hampering restrictions on foreign firms, creation of a fair tax structure and the maintenance of a stable government. After his inauguration in 1952, Tubman was "happy to confirm that Liberia's internal and external debts had been fully liquidated and Liberia at the present time was master of her fiscal affairs."

There is also growing evidence of employment interest outside the government by Liberians themselves. The transition period is marked by the phenomenon of many persons holding both government jobs and private jobs. It is likely that as soon as private endeavors become profitable, government service will be dropped by many. It is interesting to note that many of these entrepreneurs own small farms in preference to small businesses.

To augment the development of social services, President Tubman has used the United Nations organizations, WHO, UNICEF and UNESCO. Foreign companies also provide social services for employees. He is particularly interested in public health and education. Much, if not all, of Liberia's health and education facilities had been in missionary hands. The government supports many missionary endeavors but is also trying to improve the state system. Tubman feels education is the key to development and has concentrated on improving educational opportunities, particularly teacher training and technical training including administrative skills. Liberia lacked the cadre of European civil servants who could impart discipline and standards to their African counterparts. Consequently, he has been sending increasing numbers of Liberian young people to foreign universities for training and then pushing them immediately into administrative positions and advancing them as rapidly as possible. Liberia's educational budget has risen from $83,000 dollars in the 1940's to over $2,000,000 in 1959.

There is really no effective opposition to the president. He is recognized by the overwhelming majority as the savior of his country. The opposition that exists seems to come from the small extreme left and right wings.

The great social change that occurred during the first years of his administration was clearly the result of his own determination to bring about this change. An address he gave several years ago reflects this determination. He said, in part:

We must now destroy all ideologies that tend to divide us. Americo-Liberianism must be forgotten and all of us must register a new era of justice, equality, fair dealing and equal opportunity for everyone from every part of the country, regardless of tribe, clan, section, element, creed or economic status.

In the same address, he went on to indicate that he would accept no opposition to this plan.

There are still a few die-hards on both sides opposing the unification program in the hope that one element will overcome or exterminate the other. That is a fallacy. No such thing will ever happen. If any person, civilized or uncivilized, opposes the unification of this nation, he is an enemy of the state, a confirmed political lunatic and should not be followed.

The president is a man who frankly speaks his mind.

### *Tubman as a Leader Among the Independent African States*

Beginning with Ghana's independence in 1957, President Tubman began quietly to devote a good part of his time and attention to African political affairs. He increased this attention in 1958 when Liberia's northern neighbor, Guinea, received its independence.

From the start he indicated deep reservations concerning the various Pan-African unity proposals for a United States of Africa or a West African Political Union being offered by other African leaders. He described them as being "unrealistic and utopian." In his talks with visitors to Monrovia he advanced his own concept of the "associated states of Africa."

When the first West African summit conference took place at Sanniquelle, Liberia, in July, 1959, most of the European and American newspapers commented that President Tubman would be unable to obtain the support of the two other heads of state, President Touré of the Republic of Guinea, and Prime Minister Nkrumah of Ghana, who would be attending the conference. Liberian stamps described this as a meeting of "The Big Three."

Soon after the conference opened on July 16, 1959, President Tubman began to advance his own viewpoints on the kind of cooperation which would be most beneficial to the people of West Africa. In his opening speech, he set the framework for the conference.

We can be sure that this meeting will be keenly followed by our brothers in Africa, and particularly those who still live under foreign rule. What we achieve will in some measure strengthen their determination in their struggle and accelerate their march to freedom and independence.

Let me make it clear that we glory in the fact that this is not a meeting to plan and plot the subjugation and suppression of peoples or nations. It is not designed to consult upon and plan the strategy for waging a hostile political, social or economic campaign against any nation, groups of nations, or races of peoples. Nor is it intended to be preoccupied with the attainment of any selfish, national, political, social or economic predominance of any one nation or groups of nations over any other nation or nations, nor any one of us over either of us.

President Tubman then launched into a definition of what the conference should accomplish. He said:

Its primary objective is the quest for a formula or formulas to hasten and effect the liberation and independence of the subjected people of our continent; to bring unity, harmony, coherence and mutual understanding among ourselves and our brothers; and finally, to consider ways and means for contributing towards world peace and better understanding between the peoples of our continent and all nations and peoples everywhere. What better, what nobler and more beneficial objective could be conceived and pursued?

It is my opinion that a practical approach to a mutually acceptable formula should take full account of all the essential elements which make for mutual confidence, oneness of purpose, and willingness to participate in joint actions for our common good. Mutual confidence in international relations is absolutely necessary, but it can only be obtained in a climate of mutual trust, candor and honesty. There must be willingness to meet and negotiate on a basis of reciprocal respect coupled with a conscientious willingness to make wise and judicious compromises in the larger interests of the millions of our continent who are yet being deprived of their liberties and of their sovereign rights.

Toward the end of his opening address, President Tubman set forth his essential political philosophy about cooperation among the African states.

Freedom, unity and cooperation should be the noble objectives of all peoples. But these will never be assured if we fail to create the right conditions which all Africans, despite their varying customs, traditions and culture, can wholeheartedly support. Thus, in our determined search for African unity, let us endeavor to evolve that formula which will be sufficiently flexible for each nation to maintain its national sovereignty in its peculiar identity. We should show a willingness to cooperate with all African countries and peoples regardless of their choice of association.

There were several days of discussion after President Tubman's address on July 16. The outside world watched with interest as to which point of view would be accepted by the three heads of state. When the joint declaration by the governments of Liberia, Ghana and Guinea was issued on July 19, it became apparent from Principle No. 1 of the Joint Declaration that President Tubman had obtained the agreement of President Touré and Prime Minister Nkrumah to his concept of cooperation among the independent African states of West Africa. Principle No. 1 of the Joint Declaration read:

1. The name of the organization shall be The Community of Independent African States.

The Declaration went on:

2. Africans, like other peoples, have the inherent right to independence and self-determination and to decide the form of government under which they wish to live.
3. Each state or federation which is a member of the Community shall maintain its own national identity and constitutional structure.

The Community is being formed with a view to achieving unity among African states. It is not designed to prejudice the present or future international policies, relations and obligations of the states involved.

4. Each member of the Community accepts the principle that it shall not interfere in the internal affairs of any other member.

President Tubman thus designed the formula which was accepted by Guinea and Ghana for practical political cooperation among the three independent nations of West Africa.

Continuing his role as the architect of a sensible, political cooperation among African states, President Tubman, at his inauguration in January, 1960, called for an economic common market for Liberia and the new independent states in West Africa. He repeated that he thought talk of political mergers should be regarded with caution. In that portion of his inaugural address where he set forth his international viewpoints, President Tubman declared:

We consider as one of the most important and burning issues in the world today the achievement of self-determination and independence for all peoples of Africa . . . this should be considered and stimulated by all world leaders and nations as a *sine qua non* for peace. We implore those that are strong to utilize their strength to relieve all men of the unjust and heavy burdens of oppression and repression which they bear and assist in restoring and placing them on the high plane of free men enjoying the benfits and privileges of human dignity. . . . This is the legitimate aim of all men. As a means of cultivating stronger ties of friendship between Africans, we envisage an accelerated program of cultural and economic exchange between African states as a basis of lasting and fruitful cooperation. We now advance the proposals of regional, economic and trade councils with a view to:

1. Negotiating and concluding treaties and instruments of friendship, commerce and navigation.

2. Opening doors for multinational investment in enterprises which require greater funds, greater markets, greater resources than would be available to any one state.

3. Investigating and presenting proposals for regional marketing

programs of products of regional importance on the assumption that even the largest and strongest unit would benefit from additional size and strength through association with its neighbors.

4. Studying, adapting, rejecting or adopting experience in regional economic cooperation amassed elsewhere.

5. Training a sufficient number of persons and, even more, to man governments, businesses, schools and hospitals as well as other enterprises in Africa as there is no need in Africa at the present time as great, pressing and important as the need for trained people.

In his suggestion that African governments should form regional bodies for economic cooperation, President Tubman also described ways this could be done:

We propose a detailed survey of the resources for education, training and research which exists in African states and we suggest the pooling of these resources so that each nation might have access to existing institutions of education and training and contribute to their support, enlargement and improvement in proportion to its size and ability to use such an institution.

He pointed out that such cooperation could take the approach of:

1. Asking the United Nations and its specialized agencies to concentrate their efforts on those fields which the African states select for emphasis.

2. Asking those interested or becoming interested in Africa to center their assistance to such projects as:

   *a.* Helping obtain professors, teachers, etc., for this expanded educational program.

   *b.* Providing scholarships for African students to study in Africa as well as overseas.

   *c.* Helping obtain the equipment, buildings, libraries and study materials involved in such a program.

3. Suggesting to the foreign businesses operating in Africa that they work with the regional organization to plan their participation in this effort by:

   *a.* Establishing or endowing chairs for teaching and research in fields of regional importance.

*b*. Establishing scholarship programs in Africa and abroad, in some cases.

*c*. Helping with equipment, books, etc.

In concluding this part of his inaugural address, President Tubman summed up succinctly a key political reality for Africa. He said:

As Africans, we face grim imperatives. Africa is not a world unto itself but an integral part of one world. We have to make a new Africa in which all races of men live and work together in the great task of reconstruction.

There is a personal side to this problem, too. The final afternoon that I was to spend in Liberia, I visited a school operated by an American missionary group. Although small and modest, it was in many ways a beautiful place on the side of a river. The minister and his wife did practically the whole job by themselves, teaching, administering and taking care of the spiritual needs of their students. They obviously operated on a small budget.

The next morning, the same taxi driver who had taken me around for several days to visit the various technical assistance projects and had also taken me to the missionary school, came to my hotel to take me to the airport. After he had unloaded my luggage at the airport and taken care of some other matters, I paid him and gave him, perhaps, an extra generous tip because he had been so helpful. He thanked me and then said he had something that he wanted to tell me. I must in all honesty confess that I thought then that he would ask me for an extra contribution. In a moment, however, I realized that he was telling me something from the bottom of his heart. He said that he liked Americans very much—but wouldn't it be possible to send more Americans like the ones who operated the church school that we had visited yesterday? He said in his own humble English that these were the people whom the Liberians realized did not come to Liberia for money or high salaries but who came to give the Liberians something, something which was part of their love.

## An Evaluation

President Tubman has done more for the Liberian people than any man in this country's history. In his first sixteen years as President of West Africa's oldest republic, he established himself as an engaging, personable, hardworking, intelligent man possessed of a sensitive social conscience with great human understanding and immense political ability. He guided his "unification doctrine" through most difficult opposition and overcame decades of built-in resistance. His "open door" policy has been responsible for the dramatic improvement in the standard of living for the Liberian people. While much still remains to be done in this small, underdeveloped country, the favorable climate generated by the open-door policy will continue to attract more foreign capital. Recently President Tubman has emerged as a strong international leader calling for sensible cooperation among the independent African states. His two significant addresses relating to foreign affairs, first at Sanniquelle and then in his inaugural address in 1960, set forth an intelligent program of cooperation for the African people.

## The Days Ahead

Most observers believe that President Tubman's first two accomplishments, unification and the open door, are now such a complete part of the Liberian way of life that only a most unforeseen event could make any change. In visiting with the Liberian people, whether in Monrovia or a remote village, it is apparent that these two policies are now wholeheartedly embraced by the country.

President Tubman's emergence as spokesman for that group of African leaders who advocate cooperation between the independent states is recent. His initial success in obtaining support for an association of independent African states indicates that he has a large following among African leaders. In the immediate days ahead when great changes will continue to take place, he can be expected to advocate sensible policies of intra-African cooperation which should avoid much of the personal rivalries and ambitions that made Europe a battleground for centuries.

# IX

# Félix Houphouet-Boigny—
## Independence with Fraternity

During the period of great change that has taken place in Africa since 1946, various types of leaders have shown themselves as bold, original thinkers. Félix Houphouet-Boigny has not only provided dynamic leadership to his people in the new republic of the Ivory Coast but he has also developed a concept of international sovereignty that merits world consideration. During the summer of 1960 when nine French-speaking African states took their independence, the eyes of many people were on Félix Houphouet-Boigny because of his influence in West Africa. I myself was in Abidjan for the independence ceremonies in August, 1960. The transfer of sovereignty from France to the Republic of the Ivory Coast took place in an atmosphere of cordial friendship. The principal theme permeating the independence ceremonies was FRATERNITY. The Ivory Coast formally extended its hand of friendship to France and all peoples of good will.

Those who have known Dr. Houphouet were not surprised by his determination to turn the Ivory Coast into a citadel of fraternity—an independent country which would maintain cultural and economic ties with France and which would also look for the development of similar ties with other nations.

Monsieur Houphouet-Boigny presented his political position in an address before the fourth committee of the United Nations in the fall of 1957. His remarks, unnoticed at the time by most of the world, are the foundation blocs of his whole concept of international sovereignty.

We black Africans are just becoming acquainted with political life at a time when the very notion of absolute independence of nations is undergoing remarkable development. In this century each nation feels more and more cramped within its boundaries. The nations, even the largest, the most powerful, can no longer enjoy the deceptive luxury of isolation. Africa can be a meeting place among peoples—a land of reconciliation. . . . We [black Africans] cannot accept isolation. As political leaders of black Africa and whatever our political affiliations, we wish to cooperate fraternally . . . on a basis of absolute equality of right and duties.

Félix Houphouet-Boigny was born in a small village in the southern part of the Ivory Coast in 1905, the son and heir of a tribal chief. Today he holds the title of physician and is the prime minister of his country. More important, perhaps, he is the African spokesman for the school of thought which believes Europeans and Africans can work side by side in an era of growing interdependence. His political philosophy, reasonable and moderate, is quite simple as he expressed it a few years ago: "In association with France and the nations of Europe, we are determined to build our future, in hastening in every possible way, the economic progress and the social evolution of our country."

### The Ivory Coast

Since Monsieur Houphouet-Boigny is deeply loyal to his country, it would be helpful for us to know some of its particulars. The Ivory Coast is approximately the same size as New Mexico. Its population is more than 3,000,000. There are many tribes and subtribes. Most of the coastal tribes are related to the Ashanti and are thought to have arrived in the area about the middle of the eighteenth century. The peoples of the Southwest are dominated by the Krus, one of Africa's few maritime tribes. The Mossi, Dioula, Senufo and Fula comprise about one-half the population of the North. Other tribes are scattered throughout the territory.

The coast is smooth and guarded by sand bars and heavy surf. From the sea the terrain rises gently to a hilly plateau and to the west there are mountains of over 5,000 feet. The vegetation is marked by large, primeval forests which are of great importance commercially. There were foreign concessions from 1884 until 1912 when abuses led to control.

Abidjan has risen to commercial importance second only to Dakar on this section of the African coast. The development has hinged upon port facilities and a canal that connects the ocean to a lagoon. The territory produces palm oil, cocoa, mahogany, bananas, coffee in the forest belt, and manganese, gold and copper.

The history of the Ivory Coast has been without unique problems. In 1787 there were a number of protectorate treaties with the coastal chiefs. These were instigated by the British but for the most part ignored by the French government. In 1866 France offered the Ivory Coast in exchange for Gambia. But the British refused. At that time the French were more interested in the Senegal and Gambia river area than their southern posts. However, in 1888 Captain Louis Binger explored the territory about the Niger bend and secured the interior through more treaty arrangements. A year later the border with the Gold Coast was fixed and in 1891 a *de facto* border with Liberia was established. The French change of heart during these later years was precipitated by the imperialist vogue. Their grand design was to control Africa from the Atlantic to the Red Sea and movements north from the Guinea coast were part of the strategy. The North was easily controlled, but the South resisted French domination. At the turn of the century there was a bloody revolt in which three hundred troops were killed. However, by 1904 the

Ivory Coast was an integral part of France. The railroad, completed inland over 190 miles by 1913, was an effective instrument for French control. After World War II, France began to devote a great deal of attention to the development of her African territories. Setting aside for investment in underdeveloped countries a larger percentage of her national income than any other country in the world, France inaugurated the Investment Fund for Economic and Social Redevelopment of the Overseas Territories in 1948. This was guided by two principles: that the progress of the economy must keep pace with the political progress if stable conditions are to be maintained and that public investment must serve as a primer if private capital is to invest in a manner beneficial to those countries. The territories themselves made token contributions but most of the funds came from the French taxpayer. In the Ivory Coast from 1947 to 1957, $109,000,000 was received for schools, communications, livestock, forest and agricultural development, and public works in the major cities. The territory responded to these efforts by becoming the richest territory in French Africa. She consistently reported a favorable balance of trade, exporting practically her entire crop of coffee, cocoa and lumber. The plantation production of coffee and cocoa particularly provided lucrative employment for many Africans.

### Early Years of Félix Houphouet-Boigny

The first Prime Minister of the Republic of the Ivory Coast was born on October 18, 1905, in Yamoussoukro, a small village in the coastal area of the Ivory Coast. His father and uncles were chiefs. In addition to being influential through the traditional institutions, his father was also a prosperous cocoa farmer. By the time he was five years old, Félix was named chief of his tribe. He later studied medicine at Dakar and was graduated as a medical assistant. He worked in this field for twelve years. In 1940 he returned to the family plantation, by then a most profitable and extensive endeavor. His organizing abilities led him in

1944 to organize the Syndicat Agricole Africain. This was a group of Ivory Coast African planters united to defend their interests. A sharp contrast can be seen here with the background of Sékou Touré of Guinea. The SAA was also Monsieur Houphouet's political training ground. Here he obtained the hard core nucleus of supporters who stayed with him in the subsequent organization for the RDA, the Rassemblement Démocratique Africain.

In 1944 while Monsieur Houphouet was organizing the Ivory Coast African planters, another leader who later was to play a related role, General Charles de Gaulle, was active in broadening the area of African rights at the Brazzaville conference. Monsieur Houphouet, inspired by General de Gaulle's enunciation of African rights at the Brazzaville conference in 1944, was subsequently disappointed in 1946 when the Paris government did not implement all of these rights which they had given in principle in 1944. In 1946 he played a significant role in pressuring the French government to live up to its 1944 Brazzaville commitments.

*Leadership*

Over eight hundred delegates gathered from all over French Africa at the 1946 Bamako conference. There they organized a machine down to the local level. All political factions, with the exception of the Socialists, participated. Although there were branches in every French African area, the RDA was strongest in the Sudan and the Ivory Coast. The party was headed by a central committee and maintained a newspaper *Reveil.* By now Dr. Houphouet-Boigny was achieving clear-cut recognition as a national leader.

Between 1946 and 1950 the RDA was closely associated with the French Communists and voted with them in the National Assembly in Paris. The alliance was based on the RDA's battle against colonialism. From an ideological point of view, RDA was not Communist. When the Popular Front ended in 1949, RDA

was subject to severe repressive action from the French government. By 1950, however, Dr. Houphouet, seeing his party disin-
tegrate, effected a rapprochement with the French. At that time
it may have been, as some of the African leaders point out, an
opportunistic tactical maneuver but he seemed to feel that the
best interests of his people would be brought about by a policy
of "collaboration" with Paris. In the end, he was able to dispose
of his Marxist rival, Gabriel d'Arboussier, and dropped all association with the French Communist party. At that time the little
doctor defined his central political theme for the people of the
Ivory Coast as equality as French citizens. His thesis was that
since West Africans were French citizens in principle, they should
also receive all benefits of French citizenship. In addition to his
fight for political rights, he insisted on the right to economic
equality: higher nutrition, increased local trade, improved communications and universal education. After 1950, he moved
swiftly up through the French administrative hierarchy. Significant recognition of his right to serve as a national spokesman
came in 1956 when he became the first West African Negro in
a French cabinet. Within a few months he sponsored the *loi
cadre* for the development of the French overseas territories.

The *loi cadre* of June 23, 1956, authorized the government to
promote by decree the development of institutions of the overseas territories. It constituted a second stage in French policy
since the end of World War II for overseas lands linked to
France. The first step was in 1946 when territorial assemblies
were established in the territories and the right to vote was
granted to more than five million overseas citizens. The *loi cadre*
was supposed to avoid the inevitable procedural delays in revis-
ing the Constitution and would enable the overseas population to
participate in the progress of their institutions without loss of
time. The principal aim of the *loi cadre* for the overseas territories was to decentralize administration. Generally, it provided
for:

1. Increased powers for the territorial assemblies.
2. Establishment of executive councils.
3. Universal suffrage.
4. Increased Africanization of the civil service.
5. Organization of an economic development program.

During these several years as a member of the French Cabinet, Dr. Houphouet constantly pushed to bring improvements for the people in French West Africa. He drafted a plan for economic development of the Sahara; played an important role in organizing an Office of Overseas Students and establishing the University of Dakar. Behind this drive for development was the belief that unless these reforms were brought soon, chaos would develop and blood would flow in Africa.

From 1956 to 1959 Dr. Houphouet, as a member of the Cabinet, remained in Paris most of the time. Despite his responsibilities there he was able to maintain his leadership in the Ivory Coast. He was president of the major political force in the Ivory Coast, the RDA. He was the chief governmental officer and mayor of the principal city, Abidjan. Since it is difficult for many political leaders to maintain their influence at home during extended absences, some observers wonder how he was able to keep control of the political situation. My visits to the Ivory Coast convinced me that Dr. Houphouet had several important advantages working for him:

1. As the founder of RDA he had built up a series of "inner circle" loyalties.

2. His intellectual personality made him a skilled negotiator with the French and an excellent party chairman.

3. He maintained a well disciplined organization.

4. He was a symbol of the highest aspirations of his people.

The 1957 Bamako conference of the RDA proved a milestone in his career. It was held at a time when neighboring African states were preparing for independence. Despite concerted attempts to undermine his popularity at this conference, he emerged as the leader who obtained full conference backing for his four main principles:

1. French Africa wishes to remain in the French Community.
2. It wants complete autonomy in the African territories.
3. It wants more French aid to develop African resources.
4. It reserves the right of separation.

The year 1957 definitely established Dr. Houphouet as an African leader in advocating partnership as equals with the French Republic.

From 1957 to 1960 he systematically brought the Ivory Coast first, in 1958 to the level of an autonomous Republic within the Community, then to complete independence in 1960. This was done without bloodshed and extremism. It was done by a man who was determined to prove that an African state could obtain its independence with dignity and, while leaving the home of its former mentor, could remain in fraternal relationship with him.

Recognizing that a leader must provide more than promises for his people, Prime Minister Houphouet secured political independence without interrupting the French economic assistance program. France has spent 600 million dollars annually in Africa. To lose this, he believes, would be to lose present security and guarantees of consistent future investment.

In addition to obtaining independence for the Ivory Coast within a framework of continued cooperation with France, Dr. Houphouet has called for the development of supernational institutions. He is the founder of the Council of the Entente, which brings the Ivory Coast, Dahomey, the Niger Republic and the Voltaic Republic together in an economic cooperative arrangement.

Europe, he points out, is establishing supernational institutions. "Why, if not to bring about, by association and mutual aid, a more fully elaborated form of civilization which is more advantageous for their peoples and which transcends the nationalism that is too cramped, too dogmatic, and by now out of date?"

Africa, then, must discard at least the extreme effects of nationalism and actively embrace the idea of the "interdependence of
nations," he declares.

Now that the former French colonies are independent, he
wishes good fraternal relationships between France and the new
republics of Africa.

France has suppressed slavery wherever it existed and has put an
end to the quarrels which set different ethnic groups against one
another. It has given an education to the African masses and its culture to an élite. It has instituted sanitary and medical improvements
without precedent. In French ranks, in turn, we have poured out our
blood in the battlefields for the defense of liberty and we have won a
place in the history of France and of the free world. We do not want
to abandon this recent heritage. . . .

Deeply concerned about the standard of living of his people, he
has said:

These arrangements which we have chosen, and which are going into
effect now, offer assurances of stability and security—conditions that
are indispensable to the creation of an economic and social environment in which the African people can attain a standard of living comparable to that of the peoples of the great modern nations. These in-
stitutional arrangements are such as to attract investments in all forms
—imports of capital, technicians and methods—which are indispensable to our territories.

In 1959 and 1960, Monsieur Houphouet-Boigny became, in
effect, the international salesman for the French Community. He
toured Europe, visited the United Nations and the United States
to communicate energetically the realities of the French Community. Following a meeting with President Eisenhower on November 11, 1959, he said, "We are fighting for liberty and progress in the framework of the Western world. By associating ourselves with France, we want to associate ourselves with Europe
and therefore with the Western world." During this same period,

he initiated strong measures to prevent any Communist activities in the republic of the Ivory Coast. He has said that the Ivory Coast is firmly committed to the Western world; is opposed to international communism; will not maintain diplomatic, cultural or trade relations with Soviet and Communist countries. He furthermore has pointed out that he believes all the African countries must select their friends. He is one African leader who does not believe that it is morally correct to sit on the fence and/or try to play communism against the West.

In the summer of 1960, when he was prepared to take the final step of leading the Republic of the Ivory Coast to full independence and sovereignty, he reaffirmed his commitment to fraternity with the West. He also formally initiated the doctrine of economic liberalism: the Western European powers and the United States to invest and develop trade relations with his country. From an economic point of view he hopes to turn the Ivory Coast into the "Switzerland" of West Africa.

## The Future

Félix Houphouet-Boigny, Prime Minister of the Ivory Coast, has distinguished himself as the African leader who brought independence through a systematic process of rapid political evolution culminating on August 7, 1960, with full sovereignty. Now, as a chief of state, concentrating mostly on his immediate responsibilities to his own people, he is the leader of a group advocating harmony with the former metropolitan power and the development of friendly relations with other nations of the West. Statesmen throughout the West have hailed his political doctrine of fraternity as representing the hope for future good relationships between Africa, Europe, America and other areas of good will.

So far we have seen two African leaders of French-speaking states who hold essentially different points of view on the international aspects of their countries' personalities. Dr. Houphouet advocates a full independence combined with continued cultural and economic association with France—a sovereign state associated with its former mother country in a free sociocultural family. In Guinea, Sékou Touré advocates not only political but total national, cultural and economic separation from the former metropolitan power. During the past year Guinea has developed close relationships with the Communist states.

There is really not too much difference between President Tubman's and Dr. Houphouet's ideas on international relations. Liberia's President Tubman has spoken clearly on the kind of cooperation that should take place between Africa's independent states. Pointing out that Europe and other parts of the world have not yet attained the "one state" concept, he calls for realism and suggests that the African states, once independent, retain that independence and cooperate as friends. He feels that too much international politics will consume energies that should be spent on economic and social development.

Dr. Félix Houphouet-Boigny, Prime Minister of the Republic of the Ivory Coast, has dramatized the concept of complete independence with the maintenance of harmonious relationships with the former metropolitan power. We must now wait to see if the FRATERNITY of this great African leader will prevail.

# X

## Dr. Kwame Nkrumah—
## Pioneer for African Independence

When Kwame Nkrumah as an unknown, penniless young African applied for admission to Lincoln University in Pennsylvania in 1934, he quoted Tennyson's "In Memoriam":

> So many words, so much to do,
> So little done, such things to be. . . .

His country, then known as the Gold Coast, was a colony. With his few clothes and a few dollars, the man who years later would return to lead his people to independence, arrived in the United States to begin the years of study as preparation for his people's struggle. His stay in America was followed by two and a half years in England. In both countries he lived, almost as an exile, with no real support for his dreams. They were years of sorrow, loneliness, poverty and hard work.

Twenty years later, in 1957, with Tennyson's words "so much to do" still burning in his soul, Kwame Nkrumah electrified the world by leading the people of Ghana to independence, thus triggering Black Africa's passionate surge far in that direction. Ghana's star of freedom was to serve as the beacon light for the other African peoples long depressed under foreign rule.

125

### Ghana—His Country

What is the country like that has produced such a leader? Ghana was the first star to appear in the growing galaxy of new, independent countries of Africa's sub-Sahara. About the size of Colorado, it has almost 7 million people. The coast is smooth, with only occasional interruptions by highlands. In the East, the coast is backed by a grassy undulating plain that rises in steppes to the central plateau. The rain forest joins the coast but thins out in the plateau. This plateau changes from park savanna to scrub as it falls north to the Volta Valley. The climate is determined by the moist, cool monsoon blowing from the southwest and the hot, dry harmattan blowing from the Sahara. Seasonal variation depends on the movement of these air masses. The harmattan dominates the North; the monsoon, the South. As the two air masses meet, the seasons of each area become dry or rainy. The country is mainly dependent on cocoa but manganese, gold, bauxite and diamonds are also exported.

Strenuous efforts toward diversification are being made. The Volta Dam project, delayed for some time in implementation, is now under reexamination. There are high hopes for its success even though construction costs have doubled in the long delay. The opening of Tema Harbor will also be instrumental in keeping down the cost of imports.

Economists are still urging Ghana to concentrate on agricultural diversification and timber utilization. There is in this country, common to all growth potential areas that have gained their independence in the past few years, tremendous popular pressure for industrialization. The pressure is increased by the growing number of educated young people coming out of the schools who are unable to find productive work. These young men find little incentive in agriculture.

At the present time it seems that the government, fearful of the political dangers from dissatisfied "educated" young people is now concentrated on finding projects for the energies of the unemployed youth. The Builders Brigade, a reminder of the U.S. Conservation Corps of the 1930's, has succeeded in giving work to the young men whose education terminated in the middle schools. Observers of the Ghana situation feel that the government must make fundamental corrections in the attitudes cultivated in the educational system from primary school through the university so that more of the young leaders will direct their careers to agriculture—or even to business.

Although there is no certainty about the origin of the Ghana tribes and little real geographical connection between today's Ghana and the great medieval empire of the same name, there is certainly a psychological emotional bond between the Ghana of today and the ancient glories.

Local tradition holds that Semitic immigrants from the Tigris-Euphrates area established a white dynasty in the fourth century A.D. The throne later passed to a Negro family. Arab journals list twenty-two sovereigns before 622 and twenty-two after that date. The empire was at its height during the eighth, ninth and tenth centuries, with its control extending beyond the Senegal River in the west and beyond Timbucktu to the north.

The city of Ghana, focal point in the empire, grew in strength from trade and agriculture. The town, like most ancient cities of this part of the world, was divided into two sections: pagan and Moslem. It was built of wood and stone and surrounded by fertile fields. The city was the gateway to the Sudan,* and a center of trade and commerce. Its wealth flourished on trade in gold, slaves, skins, ivory, kola nuts, gums, honey, corn and cotton. Slaves were supplied by raids and conquest; gold was mined by shy tribes in the west who refused to be seen by foreigners. Silent barter was arranged by leaving the goods for approval and then retiring out of sight. These tribes managed to keep their independence by refusing to mine if conquered.

* Not to be confused with the Anglo-Egyptian Sudan in Northeast Africa.

In 1076 the city of Ghana was captured by the Berbers who placed a Moslem king on the throne as a vassal to the Egyptian caliph. Some claim that this invasion devastated the city beyond recovery; others that the change in dynasty in Ghana altered very little the habits or prosperity of the country.

In 1240 Ghana was destroyed and absorbed by Mali and the capital city of that name took Ghana's place as the richest city of Western Sudan. The Ghana-Mali conflict drove some tribes south of the forest belt. The migrations are supposed to have begun around 1200 and the senior Akan tribe settled near the coast about 1500. Most of the present tribes in the area, now known as Ghana, migrated there during the 1200–1500 period.

For working purposes we can say that the history of present Ghana began in the fifteenth century when Portuguese traders first rounded the Guinea coast in search of gold. By 1471 they were building forts as commercial outposts on rented land. The colonization of the West Indies in the sixteenth century and the subsequent demand for slaves soon brought strong competitors to the Gold Coast. By 1530 British, French, Flemish and Dutch merchants were visiting the area.

The Dutch, who soon were strong enough to gain control of most of the coastal area, pioneered the slave trade and gained a monopoly during the seventeenth and part of the eighteenth centuries. During these years the British were too preoccupied with other parts of the world to be concerned with the West African trade. But by the end of the eighteenth century the British, through their Royal Africa Company, became deeply involved. Slave exportation reached an average of ten thousand persons yearly. Dutch influence had faded away by the end of the nineteenth century.

All the European traders dealt with the coastal middlemen, the Fanti and the Accra, who jealously guarded their favored position by denying the Europeans access to the interior and keeping the inland tribes away from the coast. These power conflicts, coupled with inept British administration and vacillating British policy, resulted in an unfortunate period of sporadic warfare for European trade. However, when London abolished the slave trade in 1808 there was a turning point in British and tribal relations. Heretofore the British government had followed a policy of noninvolvement. In order to enforce the abolition decision, royal cruisers patrolled the coast and administration of the territory was transferred to the governor of the Sierra Leone colony in 1821. A year later, the British were at war with the Ashanti. Because the Ashanti wanted European goods, particularly firearms, they deliberately organized the slave trade. Not only did they wish to maintain this trade but they wished to control it without interference of the Fanti middlemen.

The high cost of preserving British influence led the government to abandon the Gold Coast. Protests from the merchants won them the right to administer "informal jurisdiction" over the coast in 1828. It was the merchants' representatives who negotiated the peace treaty of 1831 between the coastal states, Britain and the Danes (who were then active) on the one hand, and the Ashanti on the other. This document was the basis for a *modus operandi* between the British and Ashanti for forty-three years when a British attack sent the Asantehene into temporary exile and a new peace treaty was signed. The government resumed political control in 1843. In the bond of 1844 between Britain and eight coastal chiefs, the Gold Coast became a *de facto* protectorate.

British policy again became vague after 1864 when there was chaos and discontent. In 1895 British military action finally assured British control of the three areas of the Gold Coast: all territories south of Ashanti, Ashanti itself and the Northern Territories. Full control was formalized by the British government in 1901. A rapid advance toward full independence began shortly after World War II. Until 1946 the governor was the sole legislator for the Ashanti and until 1951 for the Northern Territories.

He was aided by a commissioner. In 1946 the Ashanti were admitted to the Legislative Council and elected African members constituted the majority. These concessions only motivated the people for more self-government. Their desires found expression in the formation of the United Gold Coast Convention in 1947. Here a new effort in Ghana's history began, "the period immediately preceding independence." This point in Ghana's history now merges with the life of Kwame Nkrumah.

### Early Life of the Prime Minister

Francis Nwia Kofie Nkrumah was born at Nkroful in the Nzima country which backs up against the Ivory Coast, on September 18, 1909. Every Akan child is known by the day of the week upon which he or she is born. Dr. Nkrumah was born on a Saturday so he has always been known as Kwame. Kwame's father was a goldsmith, a well-to-do man with several wives. The boy was his mother's only child and she showered all her love and affection upon him. She never allowed his father to strike him and he recalls he was beaten only once by his mother. On this occasion he had spat into a stew being prepared for the family dinner when his mother failed to give him his way.

Although his mother had no formal education, she insisted that young Kwame go to school and saw to it that he was baptized into the Catholic faith. After eight years of elementary school, Kwame became a pupil-teacher and showed enough promise to be sent to the teacher-training college in Achimoto. Achimoto was to become his political training ground, beginning with his activity in the debating club. His first position was as a schoolmaster at the primary schools in Elimina and Axim from 1931 to 1934. Here he was first introduced to real politics. This was followed by one year at the Roman Catholic seminary in Achimota where he came under the influence of Father Fraser who gave him "inspiration and encouragement."

In 1935 the future founder of Ghana arrived in the United

States to begin a ten-year period of study at Lincoln and Pennsylvania Universities where he received B.A., M.A. and M.Sc. degrees. Graduating from Lincoln in 1939, he was elected "most interesting" in his class.

This period is regarded by many as a long period of study and reflection before leadership could be openly sought. His first political action in the United States was to organize the African Students Association of America and Canada. This was the first expression of his strong feelings for West African unity. In his biography he also mentions the stimulus he received by reading the *Philosophy and Opinions* of the late Marcus Garvey, a Negro leader in the United States who attracted great interest by his "Back to Africa" movement but now is little remembered by the white population.

In 1945 Nkrumah left the United States for England. He later was to say, "It was not until the boat sailed out from the harbor and I saw the Statue of Liberty with her arm raised as if in a personal farewell to me, that a mist covered my eyes. You have opened my eyes to the true meaning of liberty, I thought. I should never rest until I have carried your message to Africa."

Shortly after his arrival in England, he began work at the London School of Economics and started his first overt political activity, becoming an active organizer and leader in the West African and Pan-African movements in London during his two-and-a-half-year stay.

### Period of Final Preparation

Finally, the time came for his return. As he approached the shores of his beloved home country, the man who was to become a symbol of hope for millions of Africans thought only of his mother. A devoted son, Kwame Nkrumah had arranged during his absence for a good friend to look after her. When he knew that he would be returning to Accra, he wrote his friend from London to arrange to have his mother meet him upon arrival.

The meeting which took place after so many years is eloquently recorded in his own words:

I think both my mother and I received a shock when we first saw each other again after twelve years of separation. At least, I did when I realized that her sight was failing and when I noticed with sadness that she had gone quite gray and that with age she had lost much of her former beauty. She seemed smaller than I ever remembered her, perhaps because she had become frail.

The first shock she had was when I smiled at her and she noticed my teeth. When I left her, my two top front teeth were divided by a fairly wide gap. In the United States I found this a handicap because whenever I made public speeches, it affected my delivery, especially where the esses were concerned. I therefore decided to have them removed and replaced by two false ones. The idea that one could have teeth removed and others put in their place, was quite foreign to my mother and when she missed the gap between my two front teeth, she began to wonder whether I was really her son. Then, to assure herself, she examined my hands, for she always said that she would know me anywhere by my hands.

As soon as she had convinced herself that this was her prodigal son, her hitherto wonderfully controlled emotions broke through the barrier and, as she clutched me to her, I felt her body vibrate with deep sobs. And then like an English April day, the sun suddenly took over and we both laughed with joy. We drew up two wooden stools and lost no more time in filling in a twelve-year gap by recounting to each other all that had taken place in our respective worlds. She never asked me, and I never told her, the reason for my sudden return, neither did I discuss with her my political ideas for the future.

Although he did not discuss politics with his mother, Kwame Nkrumah lost no time in involving himself in political matters. Within a few months after his arrival in Accra, he was General Secretary of the United Gold Coast Convention movement. Leading the "Self-Government Now" movement, Nkrumah broke away from the UGCC and formed the Convention People's Party. Within a few months he organized a program of "positive action" for self-government. When he was imprisoned by British authorities for inciting illegal strikes and sedition in 1950, he had already become the leader of a people determined to acquire independence in the immediate future. Inscribed on his statue in front of Parliament today there are three phrases which guided him and which observers believe catapulted him to quick success:

Seek ye first the political kingdom and all things shall be added unto you.

We prefer self-government with danger to servitude in tranquillity.

Our task is not done and our safety not assured until the last vestiges of colonialism have been swept from Africa.

His popularity grew while he was in prison. In the first general election, held in February, 1951, he was elected to the Legislative Assembly as the municipal member for Accra. When he was released from the James Fort Prison by the British authorities, Dr. Nkrumah was received by the wildly excited Ghanians who swept their newly freed leader to the arena in Accra for the CPP celebration. Many regard this as Kwame Nkrumah's most triumphal moment for here he was baptized by his followers as their national leader. In this dramatic event, the people of Ghana openly committed their political future to Kwame Nkrumah. Thousands repeated the chant that only seemed to have one word, FREE-DOM. It was a word that would soon be heard over most of Africa.

*Period of Full Leadership*

The self-government die was cast at that momentous evening in 1951 in Accra and Kwame Nkrumah immediately set about to hammer out the political destiny of the Gold Coast. Six years later, in 1957, it became officially independent and assumed the name of Ghana. The new nation now joined the world community of independent states. In 1960 it became a republic.

In his autobiography, Kwame Nkrumah states quite simply how on September 17, 1957, he received the official word from the British Governor General Sir Charles Arden-Clarke that his people would soon receive their independence.

I arrived at Government House promptly. If there had been any doubts in my mind as to the contents of the message that was awaiting me, the look of pleasure on Sir Charles' face as I entered his office swept it away at once. He shook me firmly and warmly by the hand and then handed me a dispatch from the Secretary of State. There was, as is often the case with dispatches, a number of long paragraphs. When I reached the fifth one, however, the tears of joy that I had difficulty in hiding blurred the rest of the document. After a few minutes I raised my eyes to those of the Governor. For some moments there was nothing that either of us could say. Perhaps we were both looking back over the seven years of our association, beginning with doubts, suspicions and misunderstandings, then acknowledging the growth of trust, sincerity and friendship, and now, finally, this moment of victory for us both, a moment beyond description and a moment that could never be entirely recaptured.

The following day Dr. Nkrumah went before the Assembly and brought the great news to the Ghanaian people that Ghana would receive full independence on March 6, 1957. When shortly after twelve noon, the Prime Minister brought these words to the Assembly, the members broke out in thunderous applause. Dr. Nkrumah was observed only to smile; perhaps recalling Tennyson, he smiled because he thought a few things had been done.

In the first few years of his country's independence, Kwame Nkrumah can stand on his record. Perhaps the greatest achievement of Ghana has been the establishment of national unity in lieu of the former tribal loyalties. The development of a national soul took place despite the predictions of the various experts in 1951 and 1957 that tribalism would destroy Ghana. Tribalism certainly has proved to be President Nkrumah's greatest challenge but it has been successfully met. In the early days of Ghana's existence few members of the central government would have dared to appear publicly in Ashanti. But now the President's recent tours have demonstrated not only his popularity but also the acceptance of the national state concept. The same is true in the underdeveloped North. He has successfully led Ghana's struggle against tribalism and the political influence of chiefs.

International stature is another criterion for judging Nkrumah's record. Among Africa's more than 200 million people, Ghana's not quite 7 million serve as a springboard for liberation. He once declared:

How we conduct ourselves when we become independent will affect not only Ghana but the whole of Africa. We have a duty not only to this country but to the peoples everywhere in Africa who are striving toward independence. If we can make a success of our independence, we shall have made an incalculable contribution towards freedom and progress throughout Africa.

The President's successful tours of North Africa and the United States and his leadership at the two Accra conferences have admitted him within a relatively short period of time into the strata of international leaders. He has served the international community as well as his own people. His proposal for a solution of the Middle East crisis and his negotiations with Guinea's President Touré reflect constructive international diplomacy.

His policy toward Africa is unity. He hopes union with Guinea will be the "nucleus of a union of West Africa states." Internationally he wishes to remain in the Commonwealth as a republic to "preserve the African character and mentality." In 1957 he told Vice President Nixon that Ghana would never be neutral in a cold war, but since then he has increasingly shifted toward neutrality as a policy goal. Although Ghana has no military power to speak of, Dr. Nkrumah is willing to participate in a United Nations force.

The prime need in all Africa is education and community development and Ghana is no exception. She has inherited the best primary and secondary school system in tropical Africa from the British. Under Nkrumah's administration the school system has been greatly expanded and better adapted to the national needs. The University of Ghana, which was always regarded as a strong academic institution, has now gained international acceptance.

Kwame Nkrumah is also concerned with development and he feels socialism is the best way for speedy, economic results. Capitalism, he feels, is too complicated. He sees the country developing on three levels:

In Ghana we have followed three principles—certain jobs and certain industries which can be done by private capital; those that can be done with the cooperation of private capital; and those that can be done by government.

Visitors to Ghana who knew the people in the old Gold Coast days, have commented on the optimistic, psychological climate that now exists among them. This change is reflected in various things like work attitudes. Everywhere in the country there seems to be a "push" for greater efficiency. Among the people you also see a greater desire to speak more effective English. Throughout all aspects of daily life there is visible evidence of higher standards.

The first few years of Dr. Nkrumah's administration have had their difficulties. Perhaps the best known is the "growing pains" of democracy. In this regard, Ghana has been criticized for official actions such as banning of the United Party meetings and for permitting acts of hooliganism; also for lacking a strong, stable opposition. In 1956 Nkrumah said:

The rights of all minorities should be respected. In practice this means that the opposition in the Assembly must have guaranteed opportunities of raising questions in Parliament which seem to them to be in the national interest. The government believes that the individual citizens of Ghana ought to be guaranteed by a law of freedom from arbitrary arrest and search. The government thinks that it is an essential part of democracy that there should be a free press.

The opposition in Ghana, however, has not flourished, partly due to its own lack of organization. In the eyes of the CPP the opposition has committed the grave sin in whipping up tribal feelings as the principal basis for its support. Since the majority of educated Ghanaians see tribalism as a threat to the state itself, they have little or no sympathy for the opposition for permitting what, to them, is near treason. Furthermore, an analysis of the opposition's statements in Parliament can lead only to conclusions that they reflect an extremist group.

## Tyrants

Sitting in a small restaurant in Accra, I overheard a European reporter discussing with a Ghanaian his concern about the growing "dictatorship" of Kwame Nkrumah. The European correspondent went on to give all the various reasons why he thought the President of Ghana was quickly becoming a one-man dictator. The Ghanaian listened with a great deal of patience and when the European finished, he replied, "Even if everything you said were true—and it isn't—we would prefer to have a dictator that is one of our own than a benevolent administration that is foreign."

The "prevention-detention act" has aroused a storm of protest in liberal circles, principally outside of Ghana. The act has been used to place men under detention, which has served to confirm the reservations that some had about the act which denies recourse to the courts and empowers the government to detain persons without trial up to five years. The greatest sensation occurred on November 11, 1958, when the government arrested forty-three men in Accra, charged of plotting to assassinate Dr. Nkrumah and other members of his Cabinet. Shortly after this, a leading member of the opposition declared that the arrests were a "further step in the calculated establishment of the one-party totalitarian state in Ghana." He also attacked the personality cult built up around the president.

In order to understand this situation, one must realize that

Kwame Nkrumah's popularity in Ghana has risen to the point where he is now a national institution. Simultaneous with this, the influence of the opposition has diminished greatly. The resultant feeling of frustration among the opposition has led to desperate statements and in some cases, desperate planning. The enormous enthusiastic support being given to Dr. Nkrumah and his government is a phenomenon common in other countries throughout the world—the political group and individuals which bring freedom to a people can command for many years the loyalties of the overwhelming majority of these peoples.

I was discussing this general problem with an African when he asked me a question that was friendly but which served to illuminate my thinking. "Who," he asked me, "ran against George Washington?"

Effective opposition in Ghana today lies within the CPP itself. In this party you find men strongly committed to capitalism, others to socialism. In the final analysis, the CPP government is actually a "middle-of-the-road government," reflecting the constant compromise that takes place between the widely divergent views within the party.

### The Future

President Nkrumah himself has clearly outlined some of his people's immediate problems. In an address welcoming Prime Minister Macmillan in January, 1960, he said:

The government and people of Ghana have two major preoccupations: the first is to develop this country as fast and as vast as our own resources will enable us to do, with a view to raising the standard of living of our people, and enabling them to live a much fuller life than has been possible in the past.

He went on to say:

Our second major preoccupation, which has already been given preeminence in our foreign policy, is to accelerate the process of liberation of the African continent and her people which was set in motion by Ghana's accession to independence. Because of a political situation in Africa today and the move for independence by all colonial territories, it has become necessary for Ghana to make her stand quite clear to the world, namely, that we believe that colonialism is an anachronism and should cease.

The pioneer of the independence movement in Black Africa has become the spokesman for the Pan-African movement. Fearing that a multitude of independent states will not serve the best interests of the African people, Dr. Nkrumah is an enthusiast for political union. While in the beginning he feels that the ties will necessarily be limited, like those of the Ghana-Guinea Union, he nevertheless has remained the energetic supporter of unity among the independent African states.

His position as a pioneer is secure. His success in bringing a sense of national unity and destiny to Ghana is remarkable. Faced with the pressing desires of his people for a higher standard of living, he has embarked upon a dynamic, forthright program for economic development.

Only a few years ago he was entitled, because of his preeminence as the leader of the first country in Black Africa, to be the spokesman for most Africans. He now faces other leaders like Senghor, Touré, Houphouet-Boigny, Tubman and Sir Abubakar. With the exception of President Touré, these leaders have viewpoints on the relationships of their countries with other African states quite different from Dr. Nkrumah.

Perhaps, in many ways, this is the natural result of freedom. Now independent, the African people through their leaders have set their sights on goals common to all African peoples. But the national frameworks which will be formulated for these goals may very well differ according to the customs and wishes of the people.

Kwame Nkrumah, the smiling young man who, when he applied for admission to an American college wrote ". . . so much to do" has already made a permanent mark as the pioneer who started the push for independence in sub-Sahara Africa and became the fluent spokesman for Pan-African unity.

# XI

## *Alhaji Sir Abubakar—*
## *Navigator for Africa's Powerful*
## *New Nation*

When the news flashed out that the little known African land
of Nigeria was to be free and would hold an election, many in
the outside world were excited to learn that it would assume
its independence as one of the largest nations in Africa. Nigeria's
35,204,000 population is roughly half again as large as that of
either Egypt or Ethiopia (the second and third largest); it is
more than double the size of the Union of South Africa.

### The Leader

Even before the votes were finally counted in the historic election of December 12, 1959, it became apparent that the Nigerian
people had selected as their first navigator a quiet, almost ascetic
man who had won them over to his support during the tumultu-
ous days of preindependence activity. It was also interesting to
many in the Western world that Alhaji Abubakar Tafewa Balewa
(soon to be knighted by Queen Elizabeth II) was a Mohammedan. Respected for his transparent honesty and his deeply
religious beliefs based on the teachings of the Koran, Nigeria's
first prime minister combined deep respect for tradition with a
progressive outlook. He had helped guide his country during the

140

sensitive years when independence was being negotiated with the United Kingdom. The goal had been achieved. There had been no bloodshed.

The first conference concerning Nigerian independence was held in London in 1953, the second a year later in Lagos (capital of Nigeria) and the third again in London in 1958. At the last conference, the British government undertook to grant independence to Nigeria on October 1, 1960. In his calm, cool and deliberate manner, Sir Abubakar told me that the great task facing him was to maintain an "arc of tranquillity" whereby the unity of the Federation of Nigeria could be assured. His land now includes what was once the Oil Rivers Protectorate, Northern Nigeria, Southern Nigeria, Lagos and the British Cameroons. His work, he felt, must be done in an atmosphere of calmness and dedication. Looking at me with his quiet, soft eyes, he told me that he felt that the people of Nigeria should be inspired by the example of the United States. When he had visited the United States in 1955 he saw that peoples of various races, colors and creeds could live together as citizens of one country, loyal to that country. Nigeria, which for decades had been divided into several regions, really did not face all the problems that the United States faced in its early history. He regarded this diversity not so much as a problem for the people of Nigeria but their greatest opportunity.

## The Happy People

Before coming to Nigeria, I had read an address he had given on New Year's Day, 1960. Now here I was talking to the man whose speech had so inspired me that I felt he must be included in my book even though I then knew little about him. In this address he said:

We have entered the most momentous year [1960] in the history of our country. Nine months from today, God willing, we shall be celebrating the independence of our country. The representatives of very many other independent countries will come to Nigeria to share in the rejoicing over the birth of a new nation. And what will those people see when they come to Nigeria? That is the challenge that confronts us. Will they find us properly aware of the new responsibilities which we are going to assume? Of one thing we can assure them—they will find a friendly people ready to develop friendly relations not only in the field of international politics but also in the more individual relationships which spring from trade and commerce. Then they will observe that the people of Nigeria are characterized by a wonderful capacity for happiness. This capacity for happiness is a priceless possession which we must never, never lose. Indeed, I should say that it is likely to be our greatest asset as a nation and I think that it was largely responsible for the remarkable example which we gave to the world three weeks ago when nine millions of us went peacefully to the polls and cast our votes. I think that it is a very great tribute to Nigeria as an emergent nation, that nearly 80 per cent of the registered voters managed to exercise their privilege to select representatives, and that there were no disorders at all.

The prime minister, speaking at a time when some other world leaders were threatening military activities to accomplish their goals, went on to say:

We must realize that Nigeria is emerging into a difficult world, a world in which as the country of the African continent having by far the largest population, we shall inevitably occupy an important position the moment we become independent. A country of 35 million people is bound to exert a powerful influence, especially in its own part of the world. Our slightest act, our every word, will have repercussions in our neighbors and I am confident that Nigeria will prove to be a stabilizing force in Africa and that our example will induce conditions favorable to orderly progress and development.

Spelling out the responsibilities of independence for his people, the prime minister added:

The liberty of a country, like that of an individual, must be limited to the extent that it must not make a nuisance of itself to other countries. Well, I don't think that we in Nigeria have any intention of being a nuisance to other countries and I very much hope that our example will be followed by others. But it is not enough to see that our relations with our neighbors are good. We must first see to it that there is proper law and order throughout the length and breadth of Nigeria. I promise you that everything possible will be done to ensure that honest men can go about their business without fear of suffering harm unjustly. . . . On this first day of our independent year I take the opportunity while speaking to my fellow countrymen, in all humility, to dedicate myself to the service of Nigeria, and her people. I ask you to pray for our new government that it may carry out our task honestly and diligently. To the people of Nigeria, whose representatives we are, the new government now calls. We call on you to join us in this great adventure with faith and confidence. . . . We are building the house of an independent Nigeria and we ask every man, woman and child in Nigeria, of whatever race or creed, to complete their own particular task in a construction so that from next October we may live in the house confident that it is well and surely built from its lowest foundations right up to the top of its roof. May God grant that we succeed and may He bless our land with happiness and prosperity.

Last January, after reading his message, I began to search through the newspapers and magazines in the United States. I could find little or nothing on the man who had issued this dramatic call to responsibility for his people.

### Nigeria—His Country

What kind of man is this about whom the world knew so little? Nigeria's first prime minister has a philosophy which springs from the soil of his country. To know Nigeria is a major step in knowing him.

Situated in West Africa, Nigeria embraces an area over almost one-sixth the size of the United States. Its estimated present population of over 35 million people makes it the largest nation composed predominately of Negro peoples not only in the African continent, but in the world.

Along the coast the climate is hot and humid with the mean

temperature of 80° and a mean humidity of 95°. These climatic conditions have been the chief deterrent to the development of a permanent white community. Less than twenty thousand of the present population living in Nigeria are white. The rainy season is often ten months with 100–140 inches of rainfall on the delta. Going north, however, the dry seasons increase as do the daily ranges of temperature.

The dominating feature of Nigeria is the Niger River, Africa's third largest river, exceeded only by the Nile and the Congo in size. At its mouth in the Niger delta there is a series of interlocking creeks, sluggish channels and mangrove swamps. The land rises from the delta and the coast gently into a hilly, densely forested plateau over a thousand feet. These evergreen forests gradually give way to a deciduous forest as the rain decreases. The rivers have cut deep valleys on the undulating plain and in the far north thin forests fade into arid steppes.

There are about two hundred and fifty different language groups, the main being: Hausa, Ibo, Yoruba and Fulani. The Hausa dominate the north along with the Fulani, the Ibo the east and the Yoruba the west. Most of the north is Moslem: in the south, however, the picture is less clear. There are roughly as many Christians as there are Moslems in the west, and in the east about half the people are Christians.

From the viewpoint of political leadership influence, the history of Nigeria may be conveniently divided between the Hausa and Yoruba peoples. While there are many other peoples throughout Nigeria, these two dominate the development of this area as a political entity. The Hausa states were established prior to the Moslem conversion in the thirteenth century. The original seven states were each named after their central city. Here resided the king, his council of ministers and the judiciary. Such a highly organized administration was supported by extensive trade. The city itself was a fortress against invaders. Within the walls was land enough to sustain a siege. Each state was independent but bound in a loose confederation by language and religion for purposes of mutual defense. In spite of their common cultural heritage, there was constant internecine warfare. While the states flourished between the thirteenth and nineteenth centuries, fortunes seesawed among them. During this time Hausaland was thrice invaded: by the Songhay king, Askia the Great; the pagan Kororofas from the Benue Valley and the Bronu Empire from the east.

This period of constant war was naturally detrimental to development of leadership traditions in the Hausa states. It is only amazing that under the circumstances, there was any continuance of trade and the spread of learning. That trade should have persisted under conditions so adverse says much for the commercial tenacity of the Hausa people. Agriculture probably suffered greatly as a result of these constant battles and resulted in the great famine of the sixteenth century. It was left to the Fulani uprising to dislocate seriously the Hausa way of life. This disaster, in the nineteenth century, was comparable to the destruction wrought by the Moors in the West during the sixteenth century. The Fulani, a haughty, handsome race, migrated into the Bornu states from the Sudan as early as the thirteenth and fourteenth centuries. By paying tribute to the local kings they existed as independent Moslem tribes.

A combination of political and religious difficulties led the Fulani to initiate a holy war against the Hausa whom they regarded as pagans. The Fulani were successful in many areas and established their own political dominance. Although individual Fulani rulers maintained high administrative standards, the peace was disturbed by others who abused their power of taxation and raided pagan villages for slaves. Some contemporary British accounts of Fulani rule relate cruelly oppressive and horrible atrocities against the Hausa. By the end of the nineteenth century the struggle came to an end and the area of Hausa-Fulani struggle was divided into three kinds of states: those directly under

Fulani rule; those under nominal Fulani rule although they paid a tax and acknowledged Moslem institutions; those wholly independent.

The origin of the other principal political group in Nigeria, the Yoruba, is uncertain. Legends designate their forefathers as coming from "the east." By the 1700's, the Yoruba Kingdom, which was situated in the western part of present Nigeria, was already beginning to decay. Internecine warfare, the Fulani invasion, slave raids and the British arrival all contributed to the final disintegration. European accounts are the main source of information about the Yoruba peoples. The Portuguese were the first to visit the coast of this part of Africa in the fifteenth century. They first took slaves and gold; later their trade included ivory and pepper. At the same time missionaries attempted conversions without success. By midsixteenth century British traders were active on the Nigerian coast also. The discovery of America and Spanish colonization of the West Indies stimulated the slave trade. By the eighteenth century Britain led the trade and more than half of the slaves from this coast were shipped in British ships. As the slave trade diminished, activity turned to palm oil; hence the name Oil Rivers. By 1862 Britain had occupied Lagos and established her political control there. The Berlin Conference of 1885 recognized British claims in southern Nigeria. By 1900 the British extended their political control to northern Nigeria.

British policy toward Nigeria has evolved through two stages. Initially there was a minimum of interference with the traditional authority. The British required only cooperation and the suppression of the slave trade and maintenance of conditions for increasing import and export trade. Since World War II, Britain has been actively engaged in assistance for economic development and the preparation for self-government and independence. In this policy emphasis has been placed on the new educated élite rather than traditional authority and traditional institutions.

In southern Nigeria education was largely the creation of the missions, while in the northern territories education has been the creation of the state. The emphasis is still on primary education. There will be, however, considerable development of secondary education and teacher-training facilities. Free universal primary education was introduced in the Western Region in 1955 and in the Eastern Region in 1957 but high costs have retarded the program. In January, 1957, there were about 2.5 million children attending primary schools throughout the Federation and about 80,-000 in secondary schools. The Nigerian College of Arts, Science and Technology has branches in all three regions and there are also a Technical Institute at Yaba and eight trade centers for two thousand apprentices and trainees. The University College at Ibadan serves the whole Federation, with a student body of about 1,500. And over three thousand Nigerians are studying abroad. The federal and regional governments spent 84 million pounds on education in the period of 1955 to 1960.

The first significant conference leading to Nigeria's independence was held in London in 1953. This conference decided:

1. That a federal, not unitary state, was best suited for Nigeria.

2. That regional governments would be controlled by African ministers with a premier as head.

3. That by 1956 full internal self-government was available to those regions desiring it.

In subsequent meetings held in Lagos and London it was agreed that independence would be granted to Nigeria on October 1, 1960.*

On December 12, 1959, a significant event took place in the history of Nigeria: its first national election. In some areas the voting was tabulated by the most modern method. In other remote districts the results had to be sent by camel or canoe. Essentially speaking, the Nigerian people had three political approaches presented to them through three political parties. Since the December, 1959, election would determine the first govern-

* Regional elections had taken place in 1954.

ment of independent Nigeria, the types of approaches and types of men presented to the Nigerian people might indicate some of their basic political philosophy.

The Northern Peoples Congress, NPC for short, is based in the Northern Region of Nigeria. The leader is Sir Ahmadu Bello, the Sardauna of Sokoto. It has a large following in the Mohammedan states of the north such as Kano, Katsina, Karia, Bornu, Bauchi and Sokoto. The National Council of Nigeria and Cameroons, the NCNC, has its headquarters in Lagos, the federal capital, but has its largest following among the Ibo people in the Eastern Region. The party's leader, Dr. Mnamdi Azikiwe, is himself an Ibo. The third party active in the 1959 elections was the Action Group, with headquarters in Ibadan, the principal town of the Western Region. At its head is the dynamic Chief Awolowo. He is a Yoruba. The Yoruba form the largest group in the region and provide a good number of the party's supporters. There are few real differences between the parties on philosophy. For instance, in the manifestoes published by each of the parties during the recent election campaigns there are hardly any discernible differences in their political policies except perhaps in external affairs where the NCNC took an opposite line to that of the two other major parties. The NCNC followed the line that a neutral attitude toward the two world power blocs was desirable. They spoke favorably of the neutralist policies of some of the Asian countries. But both the Action Group and the Northern Peoples Congress chose not only continued membership in the British Commonwealth after independence but favored close relations with the Western bloc powers.

In addition to voting for political parties and philosophies, the people of Nigeria were also voting for personalities. First, Sir Ahmadu Bello, the Sardauna of Sokoto, is presently and was at the time of the elections, premier of the Northern Region and has held that office since 1952. The Sardauna is an impressive man with handsome features. He moves with dignity and clothed in his white robes and massive blue turban he is an impressive personality. Sir Ahmadu received his education locally but has traveled widely both in Europe and the Middle East. His second in command of the Northern Peoples is Alhaji Sir Abubakar Tafawa Balewa, made Knight of the British Empire on New Year's Day 1960. Sir Abubakar, like the Sardauna, is a relatively young man. His progress to eminence is astonishing, especially in the north where birth is almost the deciding factor in any preferment. He did not belong to local nobility. Sir Abubakar's quick rise through the administrative hierarchy of the Northern Region could only have been the result of outstanding personal qualities. He is a deeply religious man and bases his conduct strictly on the teachings of the Koran. During the fall 1959 campaign activities he was quiet, simple and dignified. He constantly hammered home the necessity of the Nigerian people forging a unified state and then concentrating on their social and economic problems. A former teacher of English, he speaks it fluently and can express himself with great effect.

Quite different in character from Sir Abubakar, Dr. Azikiwe was especially popular with the members of the Ibo tribe. After studying in the United States, Azikiwe returned to Africa and established a series of newspapers. His ideas and philosophy were evident in these newspapers. He preached Pan-Africanism and the evils of man's inhumanity to man everywhere. Influenced by America's sensational journalism, his format, style and content followed the pattern. From then until 1957 he was active in the Eastern Region politics as well as the country as a whole. In that year he became involved in a bank scandal and a governmental commission found him guilty of "misconduct as a minister in failing to relinquish his financial interests in the bank when the proposal was made to inject public money into it." This shadow on his name did not dampen Dr. Azikiwe's interest in politics. He campaigned vociferously and actively in the 1959 election. As a matter of fact, many of the Western newspapers thought that all his activities indicated that he would be elected.

The fourth major political personality of the 1959 elections was Chief Obafemi Awolowo, leader of the Action Group and premier of the predominately Yoruba Western Region of Nigeria. Chief Awolowo was recognized as a good party organizer. In the election, his party was the only one which fought actively in the three regions and made an attempt to carry its appeal outside tribal boundaries. Chief Awolowo, a Yoruba, is a Methodist Christian. He is devoted to his church and his private life has been described as exemplary. Chief Awolowo held high office for more than five years and there has never been a whisper of abuse or corruption against him. He is a lawyer by profession.

Dr. Azikiwe and Chief Awolowo made numerous speeches which were recorded in the world press. Chief Awolowo adopted some contemporary Western advertising techniques including sky-writing and traveling by helicopter. The elections were held by secret ballot and were based on universal adult suffrage in the Eastern and Western Regions and the capital territory. In the Northern Region, where the ruling party, the Northern Peoples Congress, has not yet divorced itself from the old prejudice against women's suffrage, they were based on male adult suffrage only. In view of the tripartite congress, the election gave the NPC a resounding victory and Sir Abubakar, the close associate of the Sardauna, was called upon to form the government that would guide Nigeria's independence. While his opponents had adopted all kinds of new advertising techniques, the "golden voice of the North" managed to sound the political philosophy which the majority of the Nigerian people wanted during their first years of independence.

### Early Life of the Prime Minister

Mallam Abubakar was born at Bauchi, the headquarters of one of the most important of the northern emirates, in 1912. His father, Yakubu, was a member of the Geri which has an identity quite distinct from others in the emirate and is the people from which the Emir himself and the ruling dynasty are sprung.

Yakubu, a trusted official of the native authority, acted as liaison between the Emir and the head of the largest district in the emirate.

When Abubakar was four years old, his father moved out of Bauchi and settled in the small town of Tafawa Balewa situated on the banks of the river Gongola, a tributary of the Benue. At Tafawa Balewa there was a rural school, and it was here that the boy's education began. It is to his father's great credit that, in days when the introduction of Western education into the pre-dominately Moslem north was regarded with considerable sus-picion, he had the foresight and good sense to allow Abubakar to enter the school, a decision for which Abubakar himself has never ceased to be grateful.

From Tafawa Balewa, at the age of thirteen, Abubakar gradu-ated to the Bauchi Provincial School, and from there moved on to the Katsine Training College in 1928. Having obtained his teacher's certificate, he returned to his old school which had by then become the Bauchi Middle School. He remained there for many years, teaching geography and history but specializing in English. No doubt his unusual proficiency in English today dates from this time. Abubakar looks back on this period of his life with considerable affection. He was fond of children and loved teach-ing them, but already his study of geography and history was making him conscious of wider horizons and of the great events that were then taking place in the outside world. In 1944 he passed the examination for the Senior Teacher Certificate and was made headmaster of the school. In the next year he went to the London University Institute of Education where, after a year's course, he obtained the Teacher's Professional Certificate. On returning home, he was made a member of the Emir of Bauchi's Council and soon after was appointed Schools Manager of Bauchi Emirate. Later, as Education Officer, he took over supervision of all schools in the province.

Mallam Abubakar's early life was spent in the gentle atmosphere of the classroom. He loved children and his love was affectionately returned. In 1944 to 1946 there were repeated suggestions that he should now begin to devote his time and attention to the greater responsibilities facing the Northern Region and Nigeria as a whole.

*The Leader*

The year 1946 marks the entry of Mallam Abubakar into national politics, for at the end of that year, under the provisions of the Richards Constitution, he was elected by the native authority councils to represent his province in the Northern House of Assembly. Early in 1947 he was among the five persons elected by the House to represent the North in the Legislative Council, giving the North a voice in the central government for the first time in Nigerian history.

In the debates of the Legislative Council, Mallam Abubakar played a prominent and at times controversial part. The country soon became familiar with the deep, measured tones of the former Education Officer. That voice spoke, however, not merely in support of narrow regional interests but for the whole nation, urging and reiterating the need for national unity as a prerequisite for the claim for independence.

With the introduction of the Macpherson Constitution in 1952, Abubakar Tafawa Balewa was appointed Minister of Works and was among the first Nigerians to hold ministerial office. In 1953, the portfolios of Transport and Works emerged, and he was entrusted with this dual responsibility. In 1955, the two offices were again separated and he became Minister of Transport.

During his tenure of this ministry, Sir Abubakar traveled widely both within and beyond Nigeria. Outside the subjects of his own portfolio he has always shown a keen interest in the problems of Nigerian defense. Thus in 1955, and again in 1957, he was chosen to represent Nigeria on the West African Army Advisory Council, a body concerned with the defense of the four British West African territories.

When Queen Elizabeth visited Nigeria in 1956, he was one of the three members of the House of Representatives chosen to speak in support of the loyal address presented by the House to Her Majesty.

Sir Abubakar took part in the London and Lagos Constitutional Conferences in 1953 and 1954 at which it was decided that ministers should assume complete responsibilities for their departments. Thus he became responsible for the Nigerian Railway and the Nigerian Marine and it was under his wise guidance that these departments of government were transformed into corporations—the Nigerian Railway Corporation and the Nigerian Ports Authority. As Minister of Transport he was also responsible for the building up of the new organization of the Coastal Agency, and for the birth of an entirely new Inland Waterways Department.

No one has a deeper interest in or a more profound personal knowledge and understanding of the complex problems of transport in Nigeria than Sir Abubakar, and no one has worked more single-mindedly to improve and develop the country's transport system. His tenure of the Ministry of Transport saw the introduction of several daring and farsighted projects—the extension of the Apapa Wharf and of Port Harcourt. Both developments should be of greatest benefit to the Nigerian economy. The opening of the Escravos entrance to the delta ports and to the Niger and Benue rivers, a vast project, will provide a third point of access to the hinterland for ocean-going ships. The scheme for extending the railway to Bornu he sees as one of special importance to the future prosperity of the northeastern provinces.

### Compliment for the United States

In September, 1955, his interests in inland water transport took him to the United States where he studied the great transport system on the Mississippi and Ohio rivers. There, in the heart of the Deep South he was given a warm welcome and he looks back with particular pride to his visit to New Orleans of which he was made an honorary citizen. Alhaji Abubakar, always a keen observer, became especially interested in the pluralistic political system that had been developed in the United States. He noted that peoples of all races, colors and creeds live together as equal citizens all under the same Constitution, all with same citizenship responsibilities, duties and privileges. He was later to say that here he became inspired for the goals that he would set for Nigeria—unity with one citizenship, one set of responsibilities, one set of privileges.

In May, 1957, he went to the important Constitutional Conference in London. Among other important decisions reached, it was agreed that Nigeria should have a federal prime minister during the several years of preparation to October 1, 1960. As soon as the London conference was over he made the pilgrimage to Mecca, a duty which, as a devout Moslem, he had long wanted to undertake.

## As the Navigator

Soon after it became clear that the Northern Peoples Congress Party had secured the greatest number of seats in the federal election held on December 12, 1959. Alhaji Abubakar Tafawa Balewa, deputy leader and parliamentary leader of the party, accepted appointment as prime minister to form a government. With his usual zeal, the prime minister promptly introduced a motion requesting the British government "as soon as practical to introduce legislation into the Parliament of the United Kingdom providing for the establishment of a Federation of Nigeria on October 1, 1960, as an independent sovereign state." The motion went on to request the British government at the appropriate time "to support with the other member governments of the Commonwealth, Nigeria's desire to become a member of the Commonwealth." Thus the prime minister who during the campaign preached independence and then cooperation with Britain and other members of the Commonwealth saw his ideal realized and introduced a resolution within a few days after being reappointed prime minister. In order to discourage any premature joyous celebrations the prime minister said that the occasion was a solemn one because it meant that Nigeria was about to take upon itself the responsibility to shape its own destiny and that in the future the people of Nigeria "will not be entitled to rely on outside assistance." He told the House that the debate and the motion differed from the previous debates on the subject of self-government and independence and he described the difference as being "terribly significant." "On the two previous occasions," the prime minister said, "the motions in the House of Representatives were a challenge to the United Kingdom government—a challenge by Nigerians to the controlling power. This time it is the other way around. The United Kingdom government has challenged Nigeria."

In this first major address after his reappointment he expressed his confidence that Nigeria is ready for independence but he warned that the occasion was not a formality nor just a forerunner of independence celebrations. "It is," he said, "a solemn undertaking given publicly to our countrymen that we feel confident that we feel able to manage our own affairs prudently and justly."

Nigeria, he said, would assume responsibility for two vital subjects: defense and external affairs. "Both of these subjects are vitally important," he said, "and our assumption of responsibility for them is the full measure of independence."

He pointed out that while Nigeria is a peaceful country without territorial ambitions and with no intentions of attacking anyone, the situations in countries bordering Nigeria could give rise to border incidents and to serious misunderstandings between Nigeria and her neighbors. "Over the past year or so," said the prime minister, "there has been a good deal of trouble going on in some of the countries which border on Nigeria. As I see it, the danger is that dissatisfied elements in those countries will come over the Nigerian border to hide and will carry out sporadic raids on their own country." Again speaking a note of caution and a plea for prudence, he said, "It is my earnest hope that the visible strength of Nigeria will have a stabilizing effect on this part of the world and that our neighbors will settle down to enjoy the fruits of orderly government."

On external affairs the prime minister warned the House that the conduct of foreign relations would not be easy and did not rest on the establishment of embassies overseas or membership in the United Nations to symbolize Nigeria's political maturity. In the United Nations he said, "Nigeria will have a wonderful opportunity to speak for the continent of Africa. Provided that he is supported by united Nigeria, our representative will be able to wield an immense influence." He went on to stress that "no country can afford to have an inflexible foreign policy and whatever foreign policy Nigeria may adopt after independence, it will have to be capable of being adapted to the changing circumstances of the world."

Speaking about Nigeria's intention to remain within the Commonwealth, the prime minister paid tribute to the various elements which have contributed to the progress of Nigeria toward independence. On the road of political and economic development he hoped "that we shall find the British still walking alongside." He said that continued Commonwealth relationship would help in development of the country and lead to "investments both of money and technical skill" while the other Commonwealth countries would be able to represent Nigeria's interests where the country cannot be directly represented.

Thus the navigator of one of Africa's largest independent countries set the calm, cool and deliberate course that he had maintained in his previous activities.

Shortly after midnight on September 30, 1960, when the Union Jack, signifying a century of British rule, was lowered and the Nigerian officials hoisted their green and white flag amid scenes of rejoicing, the calm, dedicated navigator for Nigeria could reflect for a moment on his success in bringing independence with honor to his people.

## The Road Ahead

Now that Nigeria has achieved its independence the prime minister must navigate his Ship of State in such a manner as to accomplish the following goals:

1. An arc of tranquillity must be maintained so that the unity of the Federation becomes a reality. This task will not be an easy one. The three regions must climb above various prejudices if unity is to be accomplished. There are those who doubt that it can be done. If Nigeria can maintain this unity and forge a powerful state she will be one of the greatest geopolitical forces in the Afro-Asian group. Alhaji Sir Abubaker feels confident that the Nigerian people will recognize this as one of their greatest opportunities.

2. There must be continued social and economic progress. While much has been done dramatically to elevate the social and economic conditions of the people, much remains to be done. The majority of the people, for example, are still illiterate. Disease still takes a heavy toll. In this regard the prime minister stresses that unity and devotion of energies to the immediate problems of the Nigerian people will be a far more valuable service than engaging in political debates. Harmonious relationships should be maintained with the other African nations and nations throughout the world. The above goals would be difficult enough to accomplish if they were not complicated by the additional factor of international communism. The Nigerian people, firm in religious traditions, whether Moslem or Christian, do not offer a fertile market for the Communists. Unfortunately, Communists have been active in various ways to foment political dissension and to create a climate of dissatisfaction among the people. A great problem facing the prime minister will be to prevent the spreading of this vicious and destructive work.

The prime minister's determination to see that these goals are accomplished is reflected in part in an address which he gave on January 13, 1960, on the occasion of welcoming Mr. Harold Macmillan, the prime minister of the United Kingdom.

The past few years we have seen quite a number of countries gain their independence and set off under a constitution based on the parliamentary system. We have been very sorry to see in a number of cases that after a few years of parliamentary democracy there has been a complete breakdown of government and power has been seized by one section of the community. Now, it is quite clear that there has been a fault somewhere. It is easy enough to say that the countries affected were not really ripe for independence but I think that is a poor argument. The truth lies elsewhere and it seems to me that in those unhappy countries it is the political leaders who have failed their people.

This is one political leader who does not plan to make this mistake.

### An Evaluation

The realities of political power—land and people—give Nigeria the unique opportunity to become the most powerful nation in West Africa. With its population, its size and its seacoast, the country has tremendous incentives to overcome the obstacles of tribal and religious differences and convert itself into a unified national state.

Alhaji Sir Abubakar has resolved to direct this nation under an "arc of tranquillity." During the years in which he has been a leader he has emphasized the importance of developing firm national institutions. In a nation composed of differing parts, he has laid stress on unity. Every citizen, whatever his tribe or his district, must be first a Nigerian.

In the field of foreign relations, Sir Abubakar's apparent outlook seems to be one where deeds will count more than words. Nigeria, under his direction, may contribute to the welfare of

Africa by standing strong and largely silent, saying little but exerting its pressure in the direction of national morality.

The former instructor who left the school children he loved so well is now navigator of a potentially great nation. Navigator and nation have found their way to independence. The world is watching with particular anticipation the unfolding of the next chapters in Nigeria's history.

# XII

# Important Leaders in Other Areas

Almost thirty African states have entered the world community of nations in less than twenty years. This birth rate for new nations is unprecedented in the history of the world. And it still continues. When these countries are admitted to membership in the United Nations, Africa's vote in the UN Assembly will outweigh the total vote of North America and South America combined.

During this period the techniques of news reporting and communication have made it possible for almost every aspect of the changes to be made known throughout the rest of the globe. It is safe to say that the leaders and national founders of no other part of the world have been subject to such scrutiny as have these new leaders of Africa.

In the preceding pages we have examined nine of these men and the countries they represent. There are, of course, others who have been prominent in the battle for independence during this epochal period in all human—as well as only African—history. Some leaders of the colonial powers which gave (or surrendered) independence also played vital parts for which they may never receive credit. In some instances the true leaders of the African nations are still unknown. Yet while we must wait for another volume for the space and time for a detailed survey of other notable men of Africa, there are five whom we can touch on briefly here.

## *Sylvanus Olympio—Togo*

Sylvanus E. Olympio, Prime Minister of the Republic of Togo, was born September 6, 1902, in the capital city of Lomé. His life spans four epochs in the history of his country. At the time of his birth, Togo had been a colony of Germany for eighteen years. By the time he was twelve, World War I had started and invading French and British forces had driven out the Germans. Lomé was occupied by the British until 1920 when they agreed to withdraw, giving France the League of Nations mandate over most of the country. In the course of his education, the future prime minister was, as a consequence, to learn three non-African languages. The fourth epoch began in April, 1960, when he was sworn in as prime minister of the independent republic of Togo.

By the time he had completed his education, which included study at London University, Sylvanus Olympio took a position with the Unilever Company, working first in Nigeria and later in the Ivory Coast. In 1929, he became assistant to the general manager of Unilever in Togoland. After nine years he was appointed general manager of the United Africa Company, a Unilever subsidiary.

Several years after the start of World War II, Monsieur Olympio became a vice president of the Comité de l'Unité Togolaise (CUT). Some say he was its founder but he himself generously awards this distinction to the French Governor Montagne who started it as "purely and simply a cultural organization, as innocuous as one would expect an organization founded in the somber war days to be."

With the rapid evolution of Togoland since World War II, the prime-minister-to-be became a leader in political affairs. He was a member of the Representative Assembly of Togo from 1946 to

1951 and then became a member of the Territorial Assembly of Togoland from 1952 to 1955.

Apparently by this time he was one of the acknowledged leaders of his country. At any rate, with the setting up of the United Nations he became a regular visitor to New York in the interests of Togolaise independence. In 1956 the territory became an autonomous republic within the French Community with a cabinet headed by Nicolas Grunitzky. The CUT abstained from the election which was marked by various charges. A new election, with UN observers present was held in 1958 and Olympio's CUT won thirty-six seats out of forty-six in the unicameral legislature.

Togo lies only a little north of the intersection of the equator and O° longitude, and is bounded by Ghana on the west and Dahomey on the east. Volta is to the north and the Atlantic is on the south. Its principal exports are coffee, 45 per cent, and cocoa, 30 per cent. Despite price troubles, the country was able to double its coffee production during 1959 (perhaps under the stimulus of independence) to 11,500 tons. Cocoa production also rose, to 8,000 tons.

In his main policy speech in May, 1958, the prime minister outlined his program which contains significant thoughts for a new African state as well as objectives desired almost generally throughout Black Africa.

In contrast to some lands where the authority of the tribal chiefs is regarded as being synonymous with backwardness, Prime Minister Olympio's party has stated its intention to preserve chieftaincy as the "guarantee of our traditions" and as characteristic of those roots and traditions which "all societies however rapidly and dynamically evolving must always have."

Reversing the trend that has been the bane of many more "highly developed" nations, Monsieur Olympio is decentralizing government. Certainly there is no sounder way to develop the ability of a nation to govern itself than to place executive power in the hands of local councils. This is the "first time in Black

Africa" that this has been done, he says. The move toward local self-government has been accompanied by emphasis and encouragement to various "self-help" projects.

The Olympio government has also stressed clean government and "an end to all direct or indirect corruption." It has guaranteed total freedom of speech, movement and assembly. "We are not afraid of criticism, positive or negative, for public opinion is sacred."

Education and better health facilities take a high priority in Togo. In remote areas 50 per cent of the children die before they reach the age of five.

Yet despite the frequently welfare nature of many of Monsieur Olympio's objectives, he himself declares that his "most significant pledge" is to balance the budget. Even with the one-third French subsidy removed, the 1960 budget is entirely balanced from local resources. Prime Minister Olympio, like a number of African leaders, is acutely aware of the financial facts of life. After three years of unfavorable trade balances, Togo achieved exports equaling 114 per cent of the value of imports for the first ten months of 1959, most of this the result of drastic increase in agricultural production. It is hoped and intended that these exports will soon be supplemented by small industries developed in Togo and also by the export of phosphates.

"We seek to encourage saving," the prime minister declares. Again—"We must attract private investment necessary for the transformation of our largely peasant economy." This statement is significantly similar to words uttered by Tanganyika's Julius Nyerere. There is a refreshing realism in these new leaders of Africa. One element of this is typified in a move to introduce new methods for the "unwieldy French-type civil service, with its roots in the nineteenth century when bureaucracy was more of a hobby than a science." Skilled administrative manpower, Monsieur Olympio asserts, is too precious to be wasted on "nonproductive administritis."

This wise and vigorous leader has won the confidence of his small but nonetheless effervescent country. His Togolese Unity Committee (CUT) recently won 85 per cent of the seats in the municipal elections in Lomé. But the "outs" here, as elsewhere, are encouraged to take part in the building of the new nation. In the words of its first prime minister: "Togo is a small nation and needs all her children."

### Amadou Ahidjo—Republic of Cameroons

This African leader, prime minister of the Republic of Cameroons, was born in 1924. As a young man he studied to be a radio operator. When the winds of independence began to stir political activities in his country, he entered politics in 1946 at the age of twenty-two. First elected to the Assembly, he quickly rose through various positions until he became the prime minister and guided his country to independence on the first day of January, 1960.

Its 166,000 square miles are roughly equivalent to the state of California. The over-all population of around 3.2 million people includes around 1.7 million Christians and over a half million Moslems.

Amadou Ahidjo was the first head of an African state in 1960 who found his people the victim of terrorist attacks. During the first few months of that year some observers felt that organized Leftist terrorist activities could cause the downfall of Mr. Ahidjo's government. However, his party in February, 1960, won a decisive victory at the polls. This, coupled with strong measures by the government, have brought about greater stability in the republic. Observers now feel that as the leader of the republic of the Cameroons, Mr. Ahidjo will be able to devote his energies to the great social and economic problems that face him and his people.

## Belgian Congo Leaders

One of the most dramatic developments of 1960 was the independence achieved by the Belgian Congo. This great tropical basin, seventy-seven times the size of Belgium and rich in uranium and rubber, with almost 14,000,000 people, received its independence June 30, 1960. A dramatic aspect of this development was the special role played by Belgium's young King Baudouin who flew personally into the Congo to meet with Congolese leaders. He followed this up with a historic Brussels Conference in February, 1960, when the future of the Congo was discussed with the Congolese leaders. Within a few weeks after independence the Congo was plunged into civil disorders. The government of Prime Minister Patrice Lumumba was in and out of power. The role of President Joseph Kasavubu was not quite clear. The United Nations, responding to an appeal of the Congo government, sent troops to the Congo to assist in maintaining order. A complicating factor was the insistence of the Soviet Union on their right to intervene. It is too early to make an analysis of the problems in the Congo, but it has been an unfortunate experience for the Congolese people.

## Abdullahi Issa—Somalia

When Somalia joined the family of independent nations on July 1, 1960, there was one man, the handsome young Premier Abdullahi Issa, who had played a decisive role in making this possible.

Located on the easternmost horn of Africa, jutting into the Indian Ocean, the Somali Republic's area includes 246,000 square miles with almost 2 million people. Composed of the former Italian UN Trusteeship area of Somalia and the former British Somaliland, the country's principal exports are fruits (especially bananas) and vegetables, cotton, hides and skins. This new republic is the source of one-half the world's incense. She must import foodstuffs, textiles and machinery.

When in 1949 the United Nations General Assembly resolved that the former Italian colony should receive its independence in 1960, there were many decisive problems facing the country.

Mr. Issa, premier of Somalia, was born in 1922. He approaches the task of turning his high, dry, sun-blasted and poverty-stricken section of the continent into an economically viable state hopefully and calls for an end to "misguided pessimism."

"Certainly there are troubles ahead," says the premier. "And we know that we are poor. But we have confidence in our friends and in our strength as a free people." The premier also has confidence that the United States, Britain and Italy will supply the five million dollars annually which he estimates his nation needs to remain in business over the next several years. Most of the inhabitants of Somalia are nomadic tribesmen.

There is strong sentiment for union, Mr. Issa declares, among Somalis in Somalia and French Somaliland. There are also other Somali peoples in neighboring Kenya and Ethiopia. Such a combination would double or perhaps triple the present territory of the country. The details of such a solution, however, are wisely being deferred until after full independence has been achieved.

During the 1949–1960 period when Somalia prepared itself for independence, Abdullahi Issa became known as the peaceful mediator among the varying forces within his country, a role that many other present African leaders will be forced to play.

Now, in the first few years he faces mighty problems of turning the newly gained independence into a better life for his peoples. This will not be an easy task.

## Edward Mutesa II—Uganda

Uganda, the land of many lakes (Lake Albert is to the west and Lake Kioga and the great Lake Victoria and Lake Naivasha to the south) has one of the most attractive countrysides in Africa. Almost twice the size of New York, the Uganda protectorate includes various treaty states. It has long been the objective of Christian missionaries. The state of Buganda, although it contains only 17 per cent of the population, is politically and culturally the most significant region. The Buganda people enjoy the highest standard of living and, in the early period of Uganda administration, their chiefs were utilized by the British to help rule many of the other areas of the protectorate.

Today they consider themselves the social and political élite of Uganda—a claim well supported by the large number of Buganda who have received college and university eductation. Their claim for special recognition in the political framework of the protectorate is derived from the 1900 agreement which places Buganda on a different footing from the rest of the country. This agreement gave authority to their native ruler, the Kabaka, through his ministers, to provide directly for the maintenance of law and order and the administration of justice in Buganda. Authority was exercised through Buganda's local parliament, the Lukiko, which was made up for many years of nominated men and chiefs. Modern agitational politics in Buganda, which began to emerge in the thirties and in the early postwar period, sought a broader basis of representation and economic reforms. The riots in Buganda in 1945 and 1949 indicated that a new kind of politics, not predominantly concerned with tribal security and integrity, had evolved. The interest and expectation of new social groups had helped to produce a basis for the growth of territorially wide political action.

Edward Mutesa II, born in 1924, received his early education from Christian missionaries at Kings College at Budo. When at fifteen his father died, he was named king under a regency. In 1947 he went to Makerere College and a year later, on his eighteenth birthday, he was crowned. At twenty-one he traveled to Cambridge where he studied at Magdalene College. He is a

Christian and belongs to a family that traces its ancestry back six hundred years.

Mutesa II is the thirty-fifth Kabaka. The chiefs of the Kabaka's official constitutional advisers constitute the "Lukiko." In 1955, after returning from exile, the Kabaka became a constitutional monarch. It was thought at the time that his role would be the adaptation of tribal life to the needs of modern Africa. But since the new constitution of 1955, there have been various constitutional and political problems in this African kingdom. In many ways the Kabaka is in a royal dilemma—a survival of an ancient African kingdom in the midst of the great African push for independence. There are signs of instability and questions as to whether the institution of the Kabaka can adjust to the great changes taking place in Africa.

### Dr. Hastings Banda—Nyasaland

Nyasaland is one of the two British protectorates that comprise, along with Southern Rhodesia, the Federation of Rhodesia and Nyasaland. This country has about 50,000 square miles and approximates the size of New York State. The population is 2.6 million persons of whom 175,000 are Europeans and 20,000 Asian. Most of the Africans are of Bantu stock.

The past few years which have brought independence and happiness to so many in Africa have brought crisis, turmoil and death to the people of Nyasaland.

Dr. Hastings Banda is one of the focal points of Nyasaland's aspirations for freedom and a symbol of the struggle against poverty and illiteracy. He lives as an exile and has been associated with violence and murder. Hastings Banda was born in 1906 to a poor, uneducated Chewa family. In his youth he was converted by missionary efforts to the Church of Scotland. He received all the education that was available at that time in Nyasaland for Africans. At thirteen he ran away from home, and reputedly walked a thousand miles over the space of a year to South Africa for an education. In those early years of his life he recognized the value of an education. "Today," he said, "one does not fight with spears; one fights with knowledge."

He obtained a job in a Johannesburg mine as an interpreter for eight years and augmented his earnings by teaching Sunday school. Having heard a lecture by an American Negro educator, he was determined to go to America. With the aid of a Methodist bishop in South Africa he was able to enroll in Wilberforce Institute High School in Ohio, an all-Negro institution now called Central State University. After twelve years of study for a medical degree, Banda completed his work in Edinburgh in 1938. As a physician in London, his practice consisted mostly of lower-class workers, many of them white. Here his home became the center of young African nationalists. In 1951 he led a bitter fight against federation and lobbied endlessly in Parliament. Labor approval of federation was a blow to him. He encouraged the Nyasaland African Congress and it was probably during this time that he became a legend, a symbol of freedom exemplified by his voluntary exile from Nyasaland. At any rate, from London he became the leader of the Nyasaland Nationalist Movement.

After the federation was approved in 1953 he went to what was then the Gold Coast. There he was a close friend of Kwame Nkrumah and followed closely the independence movements there. He returned to London to protest independence for the federation, preferring instead Nyasaland's maintenance as a protectorate and exclusion from the federation. In 1958 he attended the All African Peoples Congress in Accra but was overshadowed by other delegates and overlooked for membership on the Steering Committee. Some feel that violence following his return to Nyasaland was a result of this neglect at Accra. He has continually argued against violence and it is felt that he seemed genuinely disturbed at the riots.

Following the Accra conference, he returned to Nyasaland after forty-one years in exile. He was called "Savior, Liberator, Messiah," and greeted by cries of "Kwaca! Kwaca! Kwaca!"— dawn. He was draped in a leopard skin and given a broom to brush the federation out of Nyasaland. His immediate goal was to get Nyasaland out of the federation and his future goal is an East African Federation of Nyasaland, Tanganyika, Uganda and parts of northern Rhodesia and Mozambique. This new area would be called Malawi. He further demands universal suffrage and an immediate African majority in the executive and legislative councils. The British object to his demands because Nyasaland is too poor, there are no trained Africans and they feel they would have to give Rhodesia dominion status. As the leader of the African National Congress in Nyasaland, Dr. Banda has systematically ousted any competition. On March 3, 1959, he was deported and jailed in Southern Rhodesia. Released in 1960 from jail he still maintains that his role is to continue his battle for the freedom of the Negroes in Nyasaland to direct their own political destiny.

In the opinion of some observers, he has unwisely attacked the Asians. It is, however, true that many Africans in Nyasaland and in other East African areas believe that the Asians profiteer at the expense of the Africans and prevent the development of an African "business class."

As the year 1960—the great year in Africa—drew to a close there was still a question mark over the future of Nyasaland. Dr. Banda still believes that his best strategy is to tough-talk the Nyasaland whites into conceding his demands: immediate African self-government, prompt withdrawal of Nyasaland from the federation. All attempts of Nyasaland officials to negotiate with Banda and to compromise have failed. Most observers feel that unless some kind of middle way can be found, there will be difficult days in the immediate future for the people of Nyasaland. While Dr. Banda does seem to maintain an extremist position, there are those who point out that as an intelligent person— and quite apart from his own reiterated support of nonviolence— he must know that large-scale violence is the one tactic guaranteed to lose him his goals in Nyasaland and his support in the outside world.

# XIII

## The World Looks at Africa

In Nigeria, the cry was FREE-DOM! The Congolese crowds yelled INDEPENDENCE! In Tanganyika and Kenya, the Swahili word for freedom heard so frequently was UHURU. But whatever the land or the language, the spirit of self-rule has swept at hurricane force over a continent. Africa has awakened from its slumber of centuries.

When Nigeria became independent on October 1, 1960, her more than 35 million people added to those who have joined the rolls of independence in the last few years made a total of 180 million out of the continent's 240 million people under the rule of Negro Africans. Many perils lie ahead as the structure of colonialism withers away and is replaced by Africa's young and untried national states. In addition to forging new political entities, the leaders of these countries, whose total area exceeds that of the United States, India, Pakistan and China combined, face the immense problems of illiteracy, disease and poverty.

The destinies of these African peoples depend largely on the less than several dozen leaders who have suddenly risen to worldwide prominence in history's greatest *peaceful* revolution.

By background the leaders represent a mixed group: poet, labor leader, judge, physician, schoolteacher, orator, clerk, radio operator and student. Their every action has been watched, partly because of the basic question in so many minds—whether the

African people are yet able to produce qualified leadership. Despite an often chill and unsympathetic climate, these African leaders have walked onto the world stage with poise, self-assurance and steadfast dedication to their goals. Léopold Senghor, the poet-philosopher, negotiated the intricate Mali Federation agreement with the best trained French diplomats. Sékou Touré challenged the world to assist him in conquering the three great enemies of his people: poverty, illiteracy and disease. The golden voice of Sir Abubakar has not only helped to forge Africa's large new Negro nation—Nigeria—but has been a source of strength to those African groups advocating freedom and advancement within an atmosphere of tranquillity. Julius Nyerere has enraptured his sophisticated American university audiences. Tom Mboya, at twenty-nine, led the Kenya delegation to astounding success in the tradition-steeped government buildings of London.

On what basis should we attempt to evaluate these new leaders? There is no precedent in history when the leaders of a given area have been subject to such examination and reexamination as the leaders of Africa. Certainly the standard of personal popularity among their own people can be answered by anyone who has visited Africa in the past few years. The leaders of the independent and about-to-be-independent countries have the wholehearted support of their people. If they didn't they simply would not be there.

The most dramatic aspect of the leadership is that 180 million people in approximately thirty different countries have been brought from colonial status to complete independence or self-rule with little bloodshed. Despite the pent-up frustrations caused by colonial rule, these African leaders in less than fifteen years have staged one of the world's greatest revolutions—and it has been for the most part peaceful. What a contrast their revolution has been to others in the past several hundred years which have taken millions of lives and caused untold suffering! Steadfast in their determination, the Africans who have been given the mantle of leadership have recognized their responsibilities to the world and brought about their goals without bloodshed and human suffering. They, in addition to leading independence movements, have, like Mr. Houphouet-Boigny, advanced new, imaginative proposals for international cooperation. The suffering that did occur, which was mostly in the Republic of the Cameroons and the Congo, was caused by unrecognized, repudiated extremist groups, not by the recognized leadership of the country, or by a complicated internal situation aggravated by the intervention of outside Communist forces.

In the beginning of our review of contemporary African leaders we discussed five characteristics common to great political leaders of the past. They were: character, exceptional intelligence, iron will, ability to attract the absolute devotion of an élite and a high native ability to estimate human nature.

Ethiopia's Emperor Haile Selassie I has been the living personification of noble character and iron will. Who of the world's leaders in 1936 could have surpassed his courage when he stood alone against the might of one of the most modern, twentieth century military machines?

The challenge of dynamic reform after many years of stagnation was seized by William V. S. Tubman so that the Liberian people now have a "new deal" of significant social, economic and political improvements.

All these leaders faced great difficulties in their youth to receive even a fundamental education. Dr. Nkrumah made the long odyssey to America for an education with hardly a penny in his pocket.

These men took upon themselves the great responsibility of claiming independence for their people and achieved it through nonviolent means. In this they had in some cases the willing, in other cases the grudging cooperation of the colonial powers.

Unlike the situation in Hungary or East Germany there were no tanks or bombing planes poised to strike down the fighters for freedom—and their success has been astounding.

The next step is for these new nation states to remain stable and avoid the ambitions for expansion and power that have turned whole areas of Europe into battlefields. They must find the means to grow and flourish. Frequently, if not universally, this will require the cooperation of older nations who can contribute capital for investment and the hard-to-learn skills of production and perhaps, above all, management. Let us look at this second phase for a while and see the possible future of these leaders and their states.

# XIV

## *The Road Ahead*

Africa's leaders have played a significant role in the Great Change since 1946. Self-government has now been obtained for most of the African people. What are the next immediate problems waiting to test the quality of African leadership? There is nothing new about them; they are the maintenance of stable governments and the three great enemies: poverty, illiteracy and disease.

Most Africans are incredibly poor by American standards. Their average per capita income is less than one hundred dollars a year. The continent holds around 6 million whites, about half of whom live in the Union of South Africa and the whites control the lion's share of the continent's wealth and power.

About 98 per cent of all Africans are Hamites, Semites, Bantus and other dark-skinned peoples. At least a third of the African people belong to no formal religious group. Another third are Moslems and their numbers are increasing. There is an enormous challenge here to the Christian world to increase the rate at which the continent is given the greatest gift of the Western heritage. Christianity is a spiritual blessing that often brings in its train great economic gifts. Some of Africa's greatest and gravest problems in the years immediately ahead will be moral, even spiritual, problems—not merely man's relation to man and the social desirability of helping the less fortunate, but man's relation to God in realizing his own highest potential. One of the most significant

*175*

differences between an industrial and an agricultural economy concerns matters like self-discipline and self-sacrifice. While the Christian nations have grievous faults, they have been leaders not only in industry and technology but also in their schools, hospitals, care of the aged, the insane, the orphan and the needy. Often this care has been the prelude to the prevention not only of human misery but the huge economic loss that accompanies it.

Most of the diseases known to the world plague the African people. In some areas where antibiotics have been introduced, the drastic drop in the infant death rate—especially in areas where polygamy is practiced—has resulted in a critical food shortage. The overwhelming majority of Africans are still undernourished, inadequately clothed and housed. Most Africans have no real possessions. Most of them cannot read or write.

The second great test facing African leaders stands before them right now. Can they establish a strong foundation of political stability and, simultaneously, help their people attack the triple curses of poverty, disease and illiteracy?

These leaders have already earned places in history. If they can meet this second test they will win the eternal affection of their people who today have no real social and economic security. For this struggle will in many ways be more difficult than the first. There is a joy and glory in freedom, but it does not make you rich. In this new battle they are being asked to do in a lifetime something that has taken the white races of Europe and America a dozen centuries—and still eludes a final solution.

### Political Stability

In sub-Sahara Africa—the area covered in this book—there is no uniformity of terrain, language, or civilization. Its various peoples now being released from foreign controls have but one common denominator: the desire for self-rule and the development of their own personalities as peoples.

The next political step forward is for these countries to establish firm national states which will serve the best interests of their people. Each African nation should have the right to select whatever form of government it wants and one which reflects its traditions and aspirations.

In this matter it may often be that Western-style democratic or republican forms, which differ considerably today from the systems as introduced 175 years ago, will not be appropriate for the governmental organization of the new African states. Some visiting American and European journalists have been loud in their criticisms of some of the forms of governmental organization in Africa today. They have called the heads of several African states dictators because their countries have not developed the democratic type of government common to most of Western Europe and the United States. These journalists have searched for multiparty, parliamentary systems in which the electorate may choose from several candidates. Since they did not find this form of government and saw no effective opposition parties, they concluded that Africa had replaced its foreign colonial masters with local tyrants.

This mistaken analysis has caused unfortunate confusion. Leaders are not good or bad because of the form of their government, but according to whether or not they rule in the best interests of the people. What right does any person, organization or country have to seek to dictate a form of government to the African people?

The traditions of centuries—and the practical possibilities—will have their influence on the forms of government that develop. Tribal Africa, with many regional variations, has long been governed by a chief, elder or emir (sometimes hereditary, other times selected or elected) assisted by a council of senior men. When an issue came up for decision, it was discussed with great candor by the council of "elder statesmen" presided over by the chief, elder or emir. All points of view were considered and thrashed out. When at last a vote was taken (formal or informal) and a decision made, no further discussion was tolerated. As a matter of fact, it was regarded as a serious offense to question a decision once it was made.

In addition to this tradition there is the fact that the African struggle for freedom from foreign domination has been a patriotic one in which, as was the case in the American revolution, there is no room for differences. In Africa today the organizations that brought independence are not political parties but nationalist, even revolutionary, movements.

It is my own opinion that most African states will avoid the multiparty system for the next several decades. Certainly the paralysis created in the unlamented Fourth French Republic of pre-de Gaulle days by wrangling splinter parties was not a model to be imitated. These African governments are largely pioneer governments and, as already remarked, an African acquaintance asked, "Who was the opposition candidate when George Washington ran for president?"

It is my own opinion that in most African states full discussion and debate over the next decades will be kept within one party. Other aspects of the governmental organization will also differ from European and American forms. Once a policy has been enacted there will be great pressure to follow it. Serious questioning of policies once enacted will be looked upon with the same contempt with which most persons regard treason.

### Economic and Social Needs

Most of Africa is chronically undernourished. In North Africa, inadequate water supplies and related problems have condemned millions to malnutrition. In sub-Sahara Africa, the problem is the poor quality of the food available, especially the protein deficiencies. These dietary problems, added to severe heat and humidity, are responsible for much of the lethargy and low labor productivity. There must be drastic improvements in the diet if the people are to have the energy and initiative to work for the improvements so necessary to their future.

In the economic sphere there are numerous, obvious needs. The countries covered in this book face one devastating fact: the average annual income is under one hundred dollars. This is poverty! It is also sheer lack of production which requires effort, tools, know-how and capital. Partly as a result and also among the causes there is no real industrial or manufacturing activity; the countries have insufficient roads and railroads, mediocre government services and poor communications. There are few hospitals and less than a handful of institutions of higher learning. Their banking systems are poor.

Africa's leaders are now up against the demand for economic and social progress. Freedom the colonial powers could give them. Wealth they will have to create for themselves. The parades and demonstrations that helped speed independence were stimulating and, in a sense, fun. The production of wealth calls for more persistent and usually more irksome efforts. A heavy task rests upon the new African governments to help stimulate and nurture the business and agricultural and commercial leadership so necessary to progress. They must educate, establish the priorities, resolve the differences and win popular support. It will mean a new emphasis: production rather than politics.

## Will They Succeed?

As we look into the immediate future of the African states we have only two sets of facts with which to predict the future: the historic fact of the peaceful revolution just about completed, and the determination of the African leaders to achieve new progress for their people.

The litany of health, economic and social problems facing the continent's leaders would frighten men of ordinary courage. It is the current wave of enthusiasm born of newly gained freedom that creates the passion to succeed. The continuance of this passion is absolutely necessary if these problems are to be conquered. I would like to suggest that the leaders in the industrial countries of America and Europe remember the Ethiopian boy who wanted to share his cross with his American teacher. The Western world now has a magnificent opportunity to help the leaders of the African people in the second phase of their struggle. In their attempt to win independence the African leaders had little outside help. Now, in their struggle for progress, if we do assist we shall, as the Ethiopian boy said, be sharing the cross. What better basis could there be for an enduring brotherhood between the African and all other peoples of good will?

# Index

Abidjan, Ivory Coast, 114, 116, 120
Abubakar, Sir Alhaji, 17, 139, 140–143, 149, 150–159, 172
Abubakar, Yakubu, 150–151
Abyssinia. *See* Ethiopia
Accra, Ghana, 7, 133, 137; All African Peoples Congress at, 1958, 169; conferences at, 42, 55, 135
Achimoto College, Ghana, 130
Action Group, Nigeria, 148, 150
Addis Ababa, 19, 20, 26, 27, 31, 38, 40, 44; 1960 conference at, 43
Aduwa, Battle of, 34, 35
Aezanas, King, 29
Africa: Belgian, 10–11; birth of leadership in, 14–24; changing boundaries of, 9–10; Christianity in, 3; Communism in, 3–5, 20–21; disease in, 176; East, 4–8; economic and social needs of, 178–180; ethnic and religious groups in, 175; food shortages in, 176; Freedom Day, 1959, 57; French Black, 78; French Equatorial, 78; French West, *loi cadre* in, 78; future for, 175–180; German East, 11; North, 7; per capita income in, 175; political stability for, 176–177; Portuguese, 11; religion in, 3, 6; resources of, 2, 5, 12; revolution in, 1–13; Sahara, 12, 120; size and population, 2–3, 5; social changes in, 18–21; sub-Sahara, 10, 16, 17, 126, 139, 176; in UN, 160; USSR in, 7

African Students Association of America and Canada, 131
Ahidjo, Amadou, 17, 164
Aksum, 29, 30
Algeria, 56
All African Peoples Conference, Accra, 1959, 55, 56
American Colonization Society, 98
Angola, 11
Apartheid, 1
d'Arboussier, Gabriel, 119
Arden-Clarke, Sir Charles, 134
Ashanti, 129
Ashmun, Jehudi, 98
Askia the Great, 145
Asmara, 26, 27
"Associated States of Africa," 97
Ataturk, Kemal, 15
Athanasius, Patriarch, 28
Awolowo, Chief Obafemi, 148, 150
Azikiwe, Mnamdi, 148, 149

Balcha, Dejazmach, 33
Bamako Conference, 1946, 118; 1957, 120
Banda, Hastings, 168–170
Bandung Conference of 1955, 42
Barclay, Arthur, President of Liberia, 100, 102
Barclay, Edwin James, President of Liberia, 101
Barth expedition of 1850, 86
Bauchi, Emir of, 151
Bauchi School, Nigeria, 151
Baudouin, King of Belgium, 10, 165